Basketball

Techniques and Tactics

by the same author

Basketball
Techniques and Tactics

VAUGHAN THOMAS
T.C., D.L.C., M.Sc., Ph.D.

FABER & FABER
3 Queen Square, London

First published in 1972
by Faber and Faber Limited
3 Queen Square London WC1
Photoset and printed in Great Britain by
BAS Printers Limited, Wallop, Hampshire
All rights reserved

ISBN 0 571 09523 2

© *Vaughan Thomas 1972*

To Garth and Kim

Contents

List of Players

featured in illustrations

Bill McInnes *Great Britain*

Vaughan Thomas *Great Britain*

George Turnbull *Great Britain*

Vic Tinsley *Great Britain*

Alan Williams *Great Britain*

Bob Wilson *England*

Carl Olson *Great Britain*

Bill Worth *England*

Pete Nicholls *England*

Clive Beckwith *Great Britain*

Rich Pearce *England*

Malcolm Campbell
Great Britain

Mags Moeran *England*

John Siddall *England Junior*

Bill Robson *England*

Carl Sylvester *Guyana*

Paul Patterson *England*

Jim Anatol *Great Britain*

Gary Brown *Combined Services*

Pete Siddall *England*

Vic Collins *Great Britain*

Colin Smith *Great Britain*

Dave Hemsley *England*

Ron Hextall *England*

Alan Hildyard *England*

Bob McKay *Great Britain*

Peter Shaw *Great Britain*

Terry Keogh *England*

Arthur Judge *Great Britain*

Gerry Howgill *Combined Services*

Charlie Robinson *Great Britain*

Ken Johnston *Great Britain*

George Wilkinson *Great Britain*
(Coach)

Steve Gubby *Great Britain*

Ken Charles *England* (Coach)

Tony Smith *Great Britain* (Coach)

A*

Key to Symbols
used in drawings

x_1	Attacking player No. 1
o_3	Defending player No. 3
x•	Player with ball
⸦	Player, showing facing direction and arm position
x ⟶	Movement path of player without the ball
x ∿⟶	Movement path of player dribbling
– – –➤	Path of ball without a player
*	Position of shot
⫻⫻⫻	Possible shooting area
x —❬	Player setting a screen
$_1x \xrightarrow{1} _2 \\ \quad \searrow x_2$	Numbers attached to movement lines indicate the order in which moves occur.

Introduction

I have read many books on basketball. You have perhaps not read any, or may have read even more than I have. But what are we trying to achieve, you and I? We are looking for something to help us become better basketballers—certainly. We want some enjoyable reading matter—perhaps. We want to be able to analyse and criticise someone else's viewpoint of our beloved game—maybe. A writer needs to keep these wants firmly in his mind if he is to achieve his own aims in writing a book. And what are those aims? To better basketball, to give enjoyment, to stimulate interest, to enhance his own reputation, to make money—they all have a part in that urge which eventually drags him away from the bouncing ball and towards the chattering typewriter.

Really though, why another book? Hasn't it all been said before? Of course it has, but in so many different ways and wrapped up in different glossy covers, depending on which god of the ball court makes the pronouncements, that one might be forgiven for imagining that there were as many different games of basketball as there were players and coaches. Now in one sense this is true, and books which explain systems of play based upon one type of game in one particular environment fail to be *generally* applicable. This is why so many excellently produced American texts have failed to have much effect on the Continental game. They just don't apply.

In another sense, of course, there is only one game—Basketball. Defined by international rules, following basic principles of play, exciting the same feelings of enjoyment, satisfaction, frustration, fatigue wherever it is played—basketball *is* basic. And yet I have not yet seen a book about basketball which succeeds in being basic, in getting to the very roots of the game. Such a book would be applicable to *every* environment, as useful to the player as to the coach, to the international star as to the beginner. I resolved to write this book. It had to be real, based upon my own experience as a player, coach, teacher and lecturer. Yet it had to be looked at with the eyes of a stranger, unclouded by old wives' tales, undimmed by preconceptions, unblinkered by prejudice. I could not have managed this five years ago, but my recent transition to sports scientist has forced me to re-examine many of my long held opinions in the cold light of objective analysis. Even as I wrote I found myself understanding more clearly, seeing the basic principles for the first time. This feeling was a wonderful experience for me. I hope you will share it.

During the early part of the book I have used the technique of cross referring between different pages whenever a technical concept is used. This will, I hope, help the reader to quickly refresh his memory about a particular aspect of play which has been described at length earlier in the book. In the later sections, I leave any still forgetful reader to use the index for cross referring, which is on the whole a tidier way of doing things.

This book might, I think, be fairly described as 'profusely illustrated'. I considered the rival merits of specially posed shots and normal game photographs for these illustrations, and in my own opinion the majority of artificial poses one sees in text books are so artificial as to be an inaccurate representation of the 'real thing' in the game. So I decided on game shots, and to enhance the personal nature of the book, took the photographs from my own scrapbook collected over a period of time. The extent of this period can be gauged by the changes time has made on the appearance of some of the players! To the unknowing models of basketball techniques who appear in these photographs, I extend my thanks for the specific part they play in this book.

The more complex team analyses which are dealt with in later sections are really beyond photographic illustration in a book of this type. In such cases I have not hesitated to use diagrams, and for their great understanding and goodwill in allowing such a welter of illustration I really must give my warmest gratitude to my publishers, Messrs. Faber and Faber. However, I doubt if the book would ever have seen the light of day had it not been for the patience, encouragement and typewriting ability of my wife, Christina, who has been one of the foundations of my basketball career.

I love basketball. I finally packed it in about 1962. The next time I gave it up for good was in 1968—I was too old. I shall probably finish with the game for ever next year . . . or the one after! Perhaps it's a drug—can one be cured? I'm beginning to hope not! Sport is the mirror of life, and yet it magnifies life. Troubles are bigger, successes are greater, pain is keener, fatigue more extreme, friendship's bonds tighter, rivalry fiercer. If experience is what makes a man, then the greater the intensity of that experience the stronger the personality. This book is a product of a product of basketball in particular, sport in general. How can I thank all who have contributed, since 'all' are those with and against whom I have played? The referees, teachers, coaches, supporters, administrators, team mates one year—rivals the next, will see themselves in the book. I therefore dedicate the book to them, and to my children that they may catch a glimpse of what sport has done for me, and may do for them.

Part 1 : Principles of play

Basketball is probably the leading ball game in the world as far as 'action occurrence' is concerned. More things happen per second than in any other comparable game. The word 'action' implies movement, and basketball is very much a movement orientated game. Wherever movement occurs, certain principles govern the way in which it happens, the effort needed to cause it, and the results occurring from it. Some of these principles can be called 'scientific', embracing the laws of mechanics, physiology, aerodynamics, etc., others have merely evolved empirically—they just work, though we may not know why. If by 'principle' we mean a *fundamental truth*, then a knowledge of principles of basketball can help any coach or player, in any situation and any environment, to solve the problems which make the game such a fascinating yet frustrating activity.

FUNDAMENTAL ASPECTS OF BASKETBALL	
Catching	Moving
Holding	Space
Throwing	Patterns
Bouncing	Support
Hitting	Con- and Di-vergence

Figure 1

If we look at what happens during a game—as the ball travels rapidly up and down the court, occasionally passing through the basket at either end, or making brief excursions out of bounds—we can discover that this movement, and the movement of ten players associated with it, can be categorised into a number of *basic* fundamentals. 'Aha', say the people whose battle cry is 'let's get down to the basics!' And they flash their eyes in anticipation of a nice, pat, list of things which if they go away and practice for a season will turn them into champions. They will no doubt be disappointed with my list, since it is probably much more basic than they would imagine. The first column directly involves the ball, whereas the second column does not necessarily do so.

All subdivisions of subjects as diverse as basketball tend to be arbitrary, but the only justification an author needs for his list is that it assists others to understand the information he is trying to impart. Consequently, Bouncing a ball is considered separately even though it involves Catching and Throwing. On the other hand, Throwing forms only one subdivision, even though it embraces both passing and shooting. The point is that ALL of basketball movement comes within these ten fundamentals, so that an understanding of all ten facilitates an understanding of the whole game.

CATCHING

In basketball we understand catching to mean the action of a player in intercepting the ball and gaining some degree of control over it by maintained contact. Generally the action is performed manually, and the types of catch are derived from such a variety of situations as seen in Figure 2.

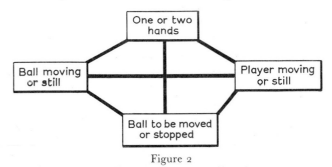

Figure 2

Even such a simple model as this shows a necessity for $2 \times 2 \times 2 \times 2 = 16$ different forms of catch, one for instance being described in such a way as:

One hand, player moving, ball moving, ball to be stopped. Whereas another could take the form of:

Two hands, player still, ball moving, ball to be moved.

15

This rather artificial classification merely hints at the very great number of ways in which good players catch the ball, and it would be time-consuming and repetitive to describe even a small proportion of them. If, however, we go back to our opening definition of 'catching', we see that the first thing to be accomplished is an interception of hand and ball. When the relative speed between hand and ball is great at moment of interception, there will be a great tendency for the ball to rebound out of the hand, and a relatively short space of time in which to obtain control of the ball. In most forms of catching, the interception method is designed to reduce this relative speed. If the ball is moving, then just before impact the hand will start to move in a similar direction to the ball. If the ball is more or less still (eg. held by another player, or at the turning point on an upward flight), then the hand will slow down just before touching the ball. In some situations, however, the time element is so short, that the movement of hand towards the ball must if anything be increased. This happens particularly when intercepting opponents' passes, or catching awkward rebounds. Naturally, one would expect there to be fewer successful catches under such conditions, but still there can be place for a last little bit of 'give' in the instant before contact. So, in the great majority of catches, the aim is to achieve a 'soft' interception between hand and ball, within the limits imposed by a given situation.

As soon as interception has been achieved, control of the ball must be developed. I use 'developed' quite deliberately, since the catcher starts with no control (before interception) and finishes with great control—he hopes. This control is not achieved immediately at impact, in fact catches which involve fast-moving balls occupy a considerable proportion of time in absorbing the force of the ball. This process itself is then dependent upon the degree of slowing down needed. For instance, if a player is moving towards basket, when he catches the ball he does not want to stop it, even if he is not going to part with it immediately. He wants to merely *adjust* the speed of the ball so that it coincides with his own speed. This is easy to do if the ball is travelling at nearly the same speed and direction as he is, difficult if the reverse is the case (Fig. 3).

Unfortunately, the easiest pass to catch is the most difficult

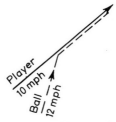

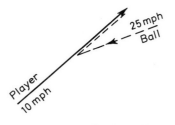

Figure 3a Easy catch   Figure 3b Difficult catch

to make (page 16), and the outcome of a successful passing/
catching situation does not depend upon making things easy
for just *one* of the two players involved!

In developing control of the ball during the catch, the total
'tension' between hand and ball is increased until it is at a
sufficiently high level for the player to be able to manoeuvre
the ball in any required manner. 'Tension' now becomes a
difficult word to define, but one could think of it as that force
which pushes the ball into the hand. For example, when a
ball is held on a single upturned hand, the tension is caused
by the force of gravity. When the ball is held between two
hands, the tension is provided by the combined force of the
hands towards one another. When the ball is held one handed
underneath the hand the tension is provided by opposite fingers
developing force towards one another sufficiently great to
cause the rough surfaces of ball and skin to lock together.

This development of tension has three basic components,
friction, force and area, all positively linked in the achievement
of catch control. There is little one can do about the friction
surface of a match ball, though steps can be taken to improve
the counterfriction provided by the skin. Drying or wetting
hands (depending on ball material), and the use of sticky
materials such as resin, usually powdered in a cloth or towel,
can do great things for a player's catching skill!

The force needed to control a catch is usually not great,
except in the case of absorbing the momentum of a very fast
pass, and is easiest to apply by two counteracting hands. In
a one-handed catch, early control is achieved *by virtue of* the
tendency of the ball to move through the hand from the force
of the pass. By pressing against the ball, the hand both slows
it down and gains control. But in order for control to be

17

maintained, that force must be replaced by some other as the ball slows down, or control will be lost.

The problem of area is the greatest one for players to solve. Obviously, the greater area of hand in contact with the ball, the more force can be applied to it. On the other hand, some parts of the hand are less flexible than others, and can sometimes *cause* control problems rather than *solve* them. The greatest area 'interface' between hands and ball is obtained with fingers spread wide and palm on the ball, this grip being maximised when the hands are diametrically opposite one another. The ball cannot be caught in this position, so the process is one of successively allowing parts to come to bear on the ball, starting from the finger tips. This gradual 'giving' with the ball can be carried on via wrist, elbows etc., if a great deal of force needs to be absorbed. The more skilful player is usually well enough co-ordinated to absorb all the force necessary mainly in the wrist and hands, without needing any exaggerated recoil of arms and shoulders.

Information

To catch a ball, a player needs information. How fast and in what direction is it moving? How fast and in what direction is he moving? Where is the ball and/or he to go after the catch? What are his team mates and opponents doing? Of these pieces of information, which all combine to a total picture of a situation, the most predictable is the ball. Quite early in the flight of a ball a skilful player can automatically work out exactly where that ball will be at the moment of catching. He will then programme his mental computer to put his hands in the right place to perform the catch, and turn his attention to the more demanding task of deciding what to do with the ball after he receives it. Just before and at the moment of contact he may not be looking anywhere near the ball, nor has he any need to. This ability can, and should, be developed by training. Film analyses show without a shadow of doubt that this is what the best players do, and scientific evidence also gives very good explanations of the phenomenon.

'Keep your eye on the ball' is certainly a good exhortation

to give the beginner at basketball, but when the player becomes more experienced and skilful such a comment can have an adverse effect upon his reaction to a total situation. Of course, if an advanced player is still fumbling catches *because* of taking his eyes off the ball, he should obviously undergo strenuous training to develop his 'blind catching' ability. A basic principle of *good* basketball is that all ball skills should be capable of being performed without looking at the ball all of the time, and that some should be capable of being performed without looking at the ball *any* of the time. The logical extension of this principle is that one spends most time looking at the ball when one does not have it in one's personal possession—but more of that later (especially its implications for the player who complains when benched '—but I hardly even saw the ball, coach'!).

Plate 1 42 (U.S.A.F. Chicksands), throwing and catching whilst dribbling without looking at the ball. Note the fingertips being last, and first, to touch the ball.

Plate 2 'All eyes on the ball—except two!' Note 7 about to make a two hand chest catch.

Typical Specific Catches

These are SOME methods of doing fairly common catches. They are not definitive. There are other methods!

1. *Two hand chest catch.* Useful for bringing ball into safe middle range working position, especially with defender behind. Arms well extended, hands pointing diagonally upwards, palms

19

forwards. First contact—thumbs and forefingers, which give with the ball, turning the palms inwards, allowing other fingers and palms to close on the ball. Give in the arms then puts the ball into a protected position, though some situations demand that the ball be kept away from the body. As this type of catch is made lower and lower down, the dropping of the arms forces a modification of the hand position until eventually the position is inverted, with the little fingers inwards and making the first contact. This position is important for scooping up low balls and bounce passes.

2. *Two hands overhead catch.* Merely an upwards extension of the chest catch, but with the wrists in a better mechanical position. In many basketball countries, this is more often used than chest catching. Combined with a jump it is the most secure rebounding catch, but the first contact might then be made with any part of the hand.

Plate 3 Bill McInnes makes a secure two hand overhead catch against Loughborough All Stars.

3. *Two hands side catch.* A sideways/forwards extension of the chest catch, with the near side arm underneath, the other arm directly above, wrists straight, first contact again with thumbs and forefingers. Usually associated with a certain degree of body turn in order to align the arms better.

4. *Two hands hand off catch.* A side catch taken closer to the body, with the near side arm above and the other below. Little fingers inwards, taking first contact. Used a great deal in close manoeuvring situations.

Most of the really great catchers perform their best when catching one handed. Understandably, this would make lesser players more prone to fumbling, but the increase in mobility and range by using just one (or other) hand has a lot to recommend it. The only balls which are really too difficult to take one handed are those travelling directly at the front middle range of the receiver. The main problem is of absorbing the force of a fast ball. In number 5 this is done by giving the hand with the ball. In number 6 the control tension is developed by *accelerating* the ball with the hand.

5. *One hand allround catch.* Arm placed in any position, using the respective arm for each body side; elbow bent depending upon distance the catch is made from body; open hand inclined diagonally towards ball; first contact with middle fingers. Ball may be transferred soon to two hands for greater security, though in many cases it might go straight into a dribble, pass or shot. Used mainly when taking passes while heavily defended, and collecting wide or high passes.

6. *One hand snatch.* Used when collecting high rebounds in a closely opposed situation. The ball is generally moving very slowly, so that as soon as any high reaching fingertips contact the ball the wrist is flexed and the whole arm is violently accelerated downwards. It is essential that the other hand makes firm contact at the lower end of the snatch, otherwise what could be a most spectacular move becomes an even more spectacular loss of control!

Catching is one of the more neglected fundamentals of basketball. Virtually everyone learns to catch as a child, and comes to the game already able to catch. Coaches therefore spend more time developing other aspects, and even when working on 'catching and passing' practices they place more emphasis on the passing techniques. But when one considers that continued possession of the ball depends in the main on catching, and that possession is vital to winning, it becomes obvious that the development of catching ability by specific training is very necessary to successful basketball.

HOLDING

In discussing catching I made the point that the ball is gradually brought under control during the catch. Eventually, (though the period of time may be very short), the ball is held in the hands and in many situations a player may need to maintain this held position for a certain period of time. The reasons for holding may be varied—allowing time for tactical development, time wasting, temporary lack of other possible actions etc.—but the situations divide really into two as far as the holder is concerned. One, when an opponent (or opponents) is trying to take possession of the ball, and two, where his possession is not disputed.

1. Disputed possession

In such cases, the holder generally finds that he has two simultaneous functions. The first, and most important, is to protect the ball from the defender. The second is to put the ball in such a position that it can be used as part of the developing offence. Unfortunately, the two functions do not normally seem to be compatible—the final development of offence tends to put the ball at risk, and this is the point at which possession is most often lost. It would be too easy to have the guiding principle that possession is the most important aspect, so that 'risky' manoeuvres are not attempted. The time limit rules for possession (5, 10, 24, and 30 seconds depending upon which set of rules are being applied) make unrestricted possession impossible. Coaches therefore have to decide upon how much 'calculated risk' is compatible with the ball holding ability of their players, and the necessity to create high scoring opportunities.

Protection of the ball is mainly achieved in two ways. The first is to use the body and/or limbs as a shield. If the ball is put into such a position that a defender's movement towards the ball tends to cause illegal body contact, then defensive movements have to take the 'long way round'—making it easy for the holder to move away from such threats (Plate 4). The second is to move the ball fairly quickly, and in a less predictable way, so that a defender cannot accurately make contact with the ball.

Holding the ball in an advantageous offensive position generally increases the risk, because a competent defender will position himself so that he is most likely to be able to thwart the ball holder's preferred offensive intentions. Since it is likely that the defender will contact the ball (and a good ball holder must assume this likelihood), the holder's tension or grip on the ball must be strong. Obviously, the strongest grip is obtained with two hands on the ball diametrically opposite one another, and with as great an area of skin contacting the ball as is possible. The hands must then develop a great pressure towards one another, which becomes easier to do if the elbows are flexed and the forearms aligned near to the line of force between the hands. Unfortunately, the more bent the elbows become, the less manoeuvrable the ball is, and different situations will demand different holding positions.

2. Undisputed possession

This occurs when a player is undefended, or where his defender is so concerned with limiting other offensive threats

Plate 4 Thomas protects the ball whilst looking for an opportunity to pass.
Plate 5 Middle working position illustrated by Bill Worth.

23

that no threat is made against the ball being held. In such cases the ball is held in positions which allow further offensive development to be made most quickly and efficiently. Generally, manual contact with the ball is limited to the most dextrous parts—fingers and thumbs. Two hands are used, because the ball can be moved quicker, and the possible variations of move are greater.

Typical Methods of Ball Holding

1. *Middle Working Position.* Strong two hand grip, ball in front of torso, generally facing opponent. Ball can be quickly put into a dribble, pass or shot. Position of greatest offensive opportunity, but also of greatest risk, so that the ball is generally moved in an unpredictable way within a circle of about 1 metre (Plate 5).

2. *Upper Working Position.* Two hand grip, ball held at any height between forehead and full arm reach, generally facing opponent. Less risk involved, therefore ball is held more in fingers and thumbs. Good for high plane passing and shooting.

Plate 6 George Turnbull protects the ball with height, in making a pass to Vic Tinsley in the key.

Plate 7 Bob Wilson has been forced into a one handed defensive working position.

Poor position from which to dribble. Can be performed one handed, using the free arm as a protective shield.

3. *Lower Working Position.* Two hands, ball below waist height. Generally the ball is at less risk, and held lightly. Good position for starting an offensive dribble, generally facing opponent.

4. *Defensive Working Position.* Any of the first three, but with back towards opponent, using the body as a shield. Arms may be bent or extended. Generally performed by closely guarded pivots, who may find defenders other than their own also trying to steal the ball from their front. In this case, pivots need to use both techniques of protecting the ball—the body against the inside defender, and the strong grip and movement against the outside defenders. The defensive working position is also used by any player who has been forced to stop dribbling and is closely pressed, but the act of turning away from basket limits the number of offensive manoeuvres possible.

5. *Rebound Hold.* Irrespective of a one or two hand catch, the hold must be made with two hands, with the ball being brought quickly into a strong position, elbows out. Within the limits of the physical contact rules, the ball is moved violently to prevent close opponents from gaining a strong grip on the ball. The body is used as a strong obstruction, often with an exaggerated bend of the trunk, though this limits the ability of releasing a quick pass (Plate 8).

There are occasions when these basic holds are not applicable, especially when conflicting offensive requirements mean that greater risks must be taken than would normally be the case. Also, unusual physical attributes may always make unusual techniques worthwhile. This is especially so in the case of very tall men who, when working close to basket, may use an upper working position almost invariably. The basic principles, however, are those which if generally applied will develop a team of 'glue pot' hands. No coach likes to have a team which continually loses possession without shooting. More attention to the development of holding techniques will go a long way towards eradicating this fault.

Plate 8 Excellent rebound hold by Gerry Howgill against Terry Keogh.

THROWING

To throw involves giving motion to a ball and releasing one's hold on it. In basketball, the principles of throwing apply to passing, shooting and dribbling. Since dribbling is an especial blend of catching and throwing, I will treat it separately but make the point that it involves merely a special use of the basic principles.

When the ball is thrown, two considerations exist for the players—speed and accuracy.

1. Speed

The ball moves because force is applied to it. This force is really a final aggregate of many forces which are added together in various ways. The amount of force necessary depends upon the speed required in the ball. In general, the basketball player wants to make his movements as quickly as possible, so this development of force is limited to the quickest acting parts of the body PROVIDED that they can develop sufficient force. If we consider the body parts which can impart force to the ball, we can see a gradual change from stronger slow parts to weaker fast ones (Fig. 4).

The position of the trunk is a special one, in that a major

26

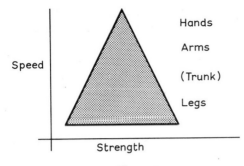

Figure 4

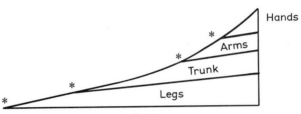

Figure 5

part of its function is to act as a link between the legs and arms, and may not necessarily be used too much to develop force. The amount of force needed to throw the ball determines how much of the pyramid is used, with the proviso that no lower section can be used without all the sections above it also being used.

In this summation of forces it is important that the slower moving parts start first, to give them enough time to make their contribution by the conclusion of the movement. An action diagram for a very speedy throw might look like that shown in Figure 5.

The precise moments when the different body parts begin their movement is extremely important in the development of force (shown by asterisks). Too soon or too late means an inefficient throw, and this secret of timing lies behind the success of those players who appear to throw effortlessly.

A second consideration in the summation of forces is the direction of the application of each force. Scientists call force a vector quantity, which means that it has magnitude *and*

27

direction. To have its maximum possible effect, a force needs to be applied exactly in line with the direction of movement required. This is rarely possible with the complex movements made by a basketball player, and the resultant force he applies to the ball (which should be in the precise required direction) may be a relatively inefficient summation of a number of forces acting in many different directions. This very inefficiency might in certain circumstances be desirable for other considerations than merely giving the ball speed. For instance, a player may want to move *away* from the basket while throwing the ball *towards* it. In this case, his leg and trunk force may be *detracting* from the total force applied to the ball, necessitating a much greater development of force in the arms and hands. During player training the coach must discover when players are experiencing difficulty in moving the ball fast enough, and analyse the possible contribution to be made by an improvement of timing and direction of forces.

2. Accuracy

When a player throws a ball, he evaluates the information about the situation confronting him, and then decides (a) how fast and (b) in what direction to throw. This decision is an extremely complex one, affected basically by the following considerations:

(a) Is there relative movement between him and the target?

(b) What is the margin of error which will allow a successful throw?

(c) Is the ball likely to be intercepted by an opponent?

Relative movement. When either the target or the thrower is moving, or when both are moving but not in the same direction and at the same speed, there is relative movement between them (Fig. 6).

In these few examples, 1, 2 and 3 all have relative movement whereas 4 does not.

Relative movement makes it more difficult to achieve accuracy, because the thrower must be able to calculate where the target will be by the time the ball has reached it (in case

28

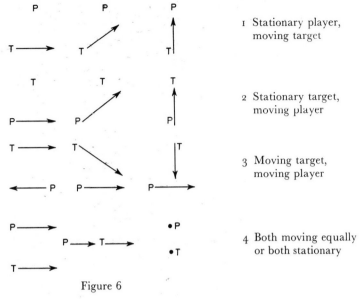

1 Stationary player, moving target

2 Stationary target, moving player

3 Moving target, moving player

4 Both moving equally or both stationary

Figure 6

of a moving target), or how much his own movement will cause the ball to move off line while travelling (in the case of a moving player)—or both!

The Margin of Error. This is the amount by which the thrower can err whilst still making a successful throw. In the case where the basket is the target, the margin of error is the difference between the apparent area of the basket and the cross sectional area of the ball. If the ball is dropping vertically this margin is at its greatest, and as the flight path approaches the horizontal the margin of error becomes smaller until it disappears altogether and it becomes impossible to score a 'clean' shot (Fig. 7).

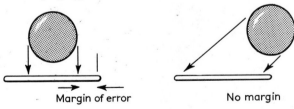

Margin of error   No margin

Figure 7

29

These considerations are further complicated by the use of the backboard, and shots which touch the ring and rebound through the basket.

In the case where another player is the target the theoretical (and usually the practical) margin of error is much greater, since the receiver of the pass can reach out a considerable distance and alter his body position to collect the ball. For this reason, the percentage of failed passes in basketball is much smaller than of failed shots, if one considers maintenance of possession as the main criterion of passing success. If, however, creation of scoring opportunities is a criterion, then a pass can be said to have failed if a good opportunity to score is not created. In such cases, the margin of error is smaller.

Interception. Within the time a ball is in flight, opponents can move and intercept the ball. The thrower attempts to select a speed and direction of movement which will not allow opponents sufficient time to move over the distance between them and the ball. If the opponent is near to the thrower, the starting position of the throw may need to be adjusted—if the

Plate 9 Thomas shooting from behind the board. Often in such positions the shooter cannot see any part of the target—only the back of the board.

opponent is some distance away, the timing and trajectory of the ball is of greater importance.

Earlier, I have mentioned the necessity of evaluating information before deciding what to do in any given situation. Apart from the considerations already mentioned, I should spend some time discussing the 'sighting' of the target. Information about the location of the target is generally obtained visually, though a team mate's call for the ball can sometimes be sufficient information with which to decide where to pass. The point is that the information does not always have to be a direct visual sighting of the target. In fact, when shooting the ball is aimed at the middle of a hole, whereas the sighting may be of a part of the ring, or a spot on the board, or even the lines on the floor. I can well remember the court in which I learned to shoot long shots—it had very low rafters, and I had to aim at a hole in the beams. If the ball went through that hole—then it would go through the ring! Naturally, the best thing to sight on is normally the target itself, but there will be many occasions when the good player has to throw accurately without looking directly at the target. In many cases, the early part of a throwing action can begin with only general information being used. Then, at the last moment a brief glance at the target is enough to make the final adjustments to the throw.

When throwing for extreme accuracy, particularly when shooting, the ideal situation is one where only height and distance have to be calculated (Fig. 8).

If, however, the ball is thrown from such a position that it is not directly in line between the eyes and the target, then a

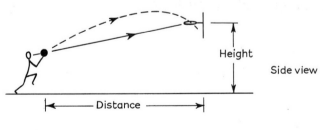

Figure 8

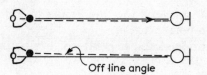

Off line angle

Figure 9

third calculation has to be made (Fig. 9). We may call this the off line angle.

Having to calculate the off line angle makes accuracy more difficult to achieve, and particularly in shooting from a long distance off line techniques are not to be widely recommended.

Plate 10 Thomas during a drive which finished with an extremely off line shot! It scored.

Force versus Accuracy

Because of the particular arrangement of nerve and muscle fibres, those movements which tend to be most powerful are also those which tend to be the least precise—and vice versa. This physiological phenomenon affects basketballers inasmuch as successful throwing usually demands a blend of both force

32

and accuracy. These effects are usually heightened when great strain is involved, because on such occasions a player may try to be powerful with his fine control parts (such as wrists and fingers), thus tending to destroy his accuracy. Within these restrictions of needing to move quickly (page 26 et seq), the necessary force should be developed by the powerful muscle groups, leaving the accuracy to the sensitive wrists and fingers.

In some cases an increase in force can be obtained by using two limbs instead of one, particularly in two-handed shooting and medium or short-range passing. For very long throws, however, a long swing with one arm is most powerful. One problem with two handed throws is that most players tend to be one hand dominant (usually right handed). It is difficult to achieve a balanced effect in this case, especially when the margin of error is small. The ideal seems to be that where the force demands of a shot are relatively small, one hand should be used for the release phase. The great majority of shots in top class basketball are made with one hand only—the very best players being able to use *either* hand singly with great accuracy.

Follow Through

All I have said previously indicates that the fingers make the last contact with the ball, which tends to roll off the fingertips. This action automatically spins the ball. It is very doubtful that this spin is of significant effect in throwing except in a very few special cases where the spin is exaggerated. In the majority of cases, the final movement of the fingers and hand(s) continues after the release, if for no other reason than the impossibility of stopping them immediately! A great deal of nonsense is talked about follow through in sport, and coaches and players should be wary of the claims made for this or that action. It seems reasonable to assume that an efficient movement before release will result in a particular one after release, but not necessarily that the production of a particular movement after release *ensures* that the previous action was a good one.

If the learning of a particular throw has been sound, then

33

Plate 11 Thomas showing a shooting hand follow through from a running shot.

the follow through will come as a natural by-product of the throw. If, however, a player is experiencing difficulty in, say, developing the part played by fingers and hands in a shot—then an emphasis on the production of a full follow through can result in an improved touch. But it is the throw that is of prime importance, not the follow through.

Mobility

Since the ball is being propelled by the fingers, a more accurate propulsion, less probability of error, can be obtained if the position of the fingers on the ball is a balanced one. The resultant force then applied is likely to pass through the centre line of the ball. With a two hands throw the fingers position is likely to be a balanced one (apart from the imbalance mentioned on page 33). With a one hand throw, the balance tends to be struck between thumb, index and middle fingers, and very little from the other two fingers. Good control is more likely if these fingers are flexible, covering a greater area of the ball. Of course, hand size is also important, but something which is very difficult to develop!

Effective hand size can be developed by improving finger mobility with exercise, and the majority of really dextrous players demonstrate a high degree of this mobility. For instance, a player with mobile fingers should be able to put thumb and little finger in line on the ball's surface.

Having considered some of the underlying principles of throwing, I should now like to look at passing and shooting separately, discussing the more common techniques used by successful players.

PASSING

Two Hands Front Pass. Made from the middle working position (page 35). In medium and short range passes the movement starts from an elbows semi flexed position. *There should be no recoil.* The ball is pushed straight out with no forewarning, the final flick coming from thumbs and forefingers as the wrists turn violently outwards. The ball can go in any front direction, sidewards passes needing a turn of the body towards that side. In long range passes, a greater degree of elbow flexion is used, and body drive may add to the force developed. One of my favourite players, Alan Williams of Wales, could catch the ball in mid air under his own basket, turn and throw a two

Plate 12 Bill Worth at the beginning of a two hands front pass. The ball travels *forward* from here, with no recoil to the chest.

Plate 13 Pete Nicholls after releasing the ball on a two hands chest pass. Being essentially a quick continuity pass, there has been no exaggerated body lean.

hands front pass before reaching the ground—with sufficient force to hit his opponents' ring!

In spite of this being the main pass taught by most coaches, its use in games tends to be mostly for continuity passing, just keeping the ball rolling. As an offensive threat to create scoring opportunities it tends to be too stereotyped and restricting of body movements.

Two Hands Overhead Pass. Made from the upper working position (page 36). Depending on the range of the pass, the force comes from the elbows and wrists. There may be preliminary movements before the pass, in fact this is such a weak position that such movement may be necessary. The pass tends to be used over short ranges though, and particularly by and to tall players, so that a great deal of force is not necessary, and in such cases it is very wristy action with the ball being either slightly lobbed over a tall defender, or travelling direct on a high plane against a shorter defender. Many continental countries use this pass as the main continuity pass instead of the front pass, employing a great deal of elbow flexion rather like a soccer throw in. They can then switch to a penetration pass very quickly, or take a quick high plane shot.

One Hand Push Pass. Can be made from virtually any position, ball held in one or two hands. Because of the greater manoeuvrability obtainable with one hand, the possible directions in which the ball can travel are more extensive than with two hands passing. However, the force developed is less, and the pass is only used over medium and short range. The action is one of elbow extension and a vigorous wrist snap, the ball in many cases being supported by the free hand until late in the movement.

Reverse One Hand Push. Many players find the previous pass difficult for the non dominant hand, and instead use a Reverse One Hand Push. Here the arms are crossed so that the non-dominant hand is underneath the ball and the dominant hand (inverted) on the opposite side to normal. The ball may then be pushed to the dominant side. This is a slower pass, but a very deceptive one.

Plate 14 George Turnbull makes a two hand overhead pass to Vic Tinsley.

Plate 15 Reverse one hand push pass by Austrian from a shot baulked by Clive Beckwith.

Bent Arm Long Pass. Normally, the ball is thrown from a sideways standing position so that the thrower can step into the movement. The trunk is rotated and the throw initiated from an elbow flexed position. The ball is held in one hand, and the elbow leads the movement until finally extending coupled with a vigorous wrist movement. The whole action is a very natural hard throwing action such as is used in baseball pitching, javelin throwing and cricket fielding—complicated only by the size of the ball. The pass is used whenever a long throw is necessary, and is the more accurate method but also the more demanding in terms of power.

Straight Arm Long Pass. Very similar to the bent arm pass, but the arm is kept straight throughout the movement rather like a cricket bowling action. The ball can be thrown overhead or around the body, and is a much easier long pass for weaker players but lacking in accuracy.

Hand Off Pass. May be made with one or two hands. Used in situations where the players are passing very close to one another, usually when at least the passer is closely marked and is in a defensive working position. The hand(s) carries the ball to very near the point where the receiver is to catch it. If one handed, the hand is upturned, and propelled a few inches upwards with a mainly wrist action. If two handed, the hands

37

roll outwards, with the ball propelled by the minor fingers. The ball should have very little force, and might even be moved slightly in the direction being taken by the receiver to reduce the relative speed.

Bounce Pass. This is not really a separate pass, just a term which describes the path taken by the ball after the release. One might equally classify the 'Lob Pass'. There are situations in the game where the ball needs to be passed via a bounce, usually to avoid interception or to have the ball arrive at an easier angle to the receiver. There is a danger in its use, because the ball is slowed by the bounce, and its use should be restricted only to situations where it is necessary. Sometimes a pass needs to travel around corners, and a spinning bounce pass can achieve the required effect. However it is very rarely used. Usually bounce passes are made from low level positions, and the bounce should occur at the position where interception of a higher level pass would be most likely, eg. near the feet of the defender.

There are many other methods of passing the ball, most of them being undistinguishable by name, others being more specifically named—such as a *Hook Pass*. These passes tend to be produced by situations, as specific answers to perhaps

Plate 16 Pass off by baulked player to free team mate. (See plate 77, page 67.)

unique combinations of circumstances. They may be produced by mind changing, where a baulked shot is turned into a pass. They might also be unique to a certain individual—for instance, when away on a 2 v 1 fast break I used to allow myself to be stopped by drawing the defender and adopting a defensive working position in mid court. Then by tossing the ball backwards with the right hand over my right shoulder my team mate could run on to the ball and be free for a shot. This looked ridiculous, and would not be a pass to be categorised and coached. But it worked for me, and usually meant a basket being scored. The coach should develop his players' ability to create solutions to specific passing problems, based on the framework of recognised efficient passes, but adapted in all cases to the prevailing circumstances.

SHOOTING

In this era of free thinking, basketball shooting has undergone something of a revolution. It is now realised that a good technique is any one which produces a high proportion of successful shots, and with defenders in such an aggressive and intelligent mood, stereotyped shooting methods which produce good results during practice do not always work out during games. Such a wide variety of shooting methods as is used these days tends to make the classification of shots a pointless exercise. The distinctions between them are too blurred. However, I have a duty to discuss the implications and techniques of shooting, and I should like to classify shots by the way in which the defence is beaten. This tends to be by the use of one or more of four techniques:

1. Penetration
2. Height
3. Obstruction
4. Free

Penetration

It is impossible for defence to completely plug all the avenues towards basket. Penetration shots attempt to use the free

Plate 17 Thomas driving between two High Wycombe players with the whole of the body and the ball.

Plate 18 Thomas using just one arm and the ball through a small gap left by two Sudanese defenders.

avenues, the holes in the defence, which may be inherent in the form of defence being used, or might be in fact created by the actions of the shooter. In such shots, the beating of the defence is done during the preparation and early phases of the shot—the later stages and the release should be relatively free of opposition.

The defensive hole might be exploited by the player with the whole of his body and the ball, moving himself through the gap by driving towards his shooting position. Such movements are called Drives. On the other hand, a shooter may merely put one arm and the ball through a small gap, the shot still depending on penetration of defence. Since the idea of the shot is to release the ball in such a position behind the defence that they cannot reach it, the shooter must extend himself, using long arms and sometimes jumping. It is anticipated that the shot will be unchecked, so a relatively weak grip on the ball will suffice—mostly by holding the ball with one hand underneath, though two handed shots are often used.

Plate 19a and b Siamese player and Thomas illustrating two handed drive shots in situations where there is greater danger of the ball being checked.

Plate 20 Thomas using a sweeping arm action to generate force from an awkward position.

Most penetration shots are released close to basket, sometimes from positions under the ring. Since the extended arm position is a weak one, the force necessary to reach the ring needs to be obtained either from a strong leg drive, or from a sweeping action of the extended arm. In awkward positions, the backboard is often used by spinning the ball 'around corners'. Since with one handed shots, the ball can only be easily spun in one direction, the approach side to the board determines whether the spin either adds to or checks the lateral movement of the ball. The following diagrams refer to a right handed shot using spin off the backboard (Fig. 10).

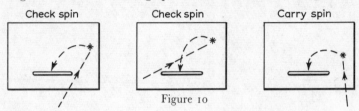

Figure 10

The point of contact can vary all over the board, and can in fact be below the level of the ring provided the ball is still travelling upwards.

The board can of course be used on penetration shots without heavy spin. In such cases, the point of contact is more restricted generally to positions higher than the ring. The ball tends to come off the board at an angle similar to the one it enters by (slightly modified by the friction between the two surfaces). Figure 10 refers to right handed board shots with spin, all of which can be made from an approach on either side. The point of spin is that it can usually be designed to give a near vertical dropping path to the ball, whereas non spin shots tend to drop obliquely. This is an important factor on drives where the ball has great lateral motion due to the motion of the player.

Some penetration shots achieve their aim by the use of sheer power on the drive. The defender may even get a hand on the ball, but if the attacker has a strong two handed grip on the ball he can push through the check. The ball can then be propelled by the force of elbow, shoulder or wrist movement —provided that the shooter has left sufficient flexion in the respective joints to produce a movement. The very great total force needed on such drives comes mainly from the leap, trunk, and shoulders—the fine adjustment after penetration coming from arms and hands.

There has always been controversy over the use of the backboard in shooting. Two opposing views are that to use the backboard involves an extra calculation, thus making aiming

Plate 21 Strong two handed penetration shot by Thomas. The defender has a hand on the ball, but by jumping strongly *through* the check, the shooter has enough flexion in his arm to propel the ball through the basket.

Plate 22 A height shot, where Thomas is the only man off the floor thus being relatively higher than his opponent.

more difficult; whereas to aim at the backboard, which is a vertical target, is easier than to aim at the ring which, being horizontal, is not clearly seen. My own view is that it doesn't much matter to the really good player *what* he aims at, he will develop great accuracy in any case. However, if he can use the board to advantage in altering the subsequent flight of the ball, then he would be well advised to do so. In making such decisions players will be affected by the type of playing equipment being used. The grip between ball and board surfaces is important in deciding how much effect the board will have on subsequent flight of the ball. Also the firmness of the board and resilience of the material effect the resultant dropping of the ball after contact. The extremely resilient backboards, and glass v. leather interface of American equipment disposes players to use the board far less than European equipment, which is usually less firm and uses rubber/nylon balls. This is especially true on the medium and long range shots.

Height Shots

This category of shot aims to release the ball from such a height that the defenders cannot reach it. It is vitally important that shooters appreciate that *absolute* height is of less importance in these shots than *relative* height (Plate 22). Provided that the ball is higher than the defender can reach, it does not matter what the actual height is (Fig. 11).

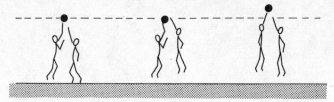

Figure 11

How may this height be obtained? Firstly, of course, by jumping— from one or two feet, from running or standing, facing to, or from, the opponent, etc., etc. Secondly, by reaching upwards as high as possible with the ball, which generally means a one handed shot since a player can reach higher with one hand than with two. These shots include rebound shots where the ball is caught and shot while in the air.

At this stage, we should consider the implications of these factors in the production of the shot. The force required to propel the ball to the ring varies with the height of the ball's flight, and the distance from the basket. The further from the basket the shot is taken, the more force is required. Therefore, the further the shooter goes from the basket, the more necessary does it become for him to involve extra propelling forces in the shot. However, the highest shot is one where the ball is released from a straight arm, above the head, at the top of a jump—in which case movement has virtually ceased, the ball is almost motionless, and the sole propelling force comes from wrist and fingers. Such a shot can only be used close to basket, where the ball may only have to travel 10–20 inches, or where

44

Plate 23 A height shot close to basket with the ball held in both hands well above the head until just before the release.

Plate 24 Malcolm Campbell with a two hand dunk shot.

Plate 25 Rich Pearce beats his defender with a medium range height shot, having released the ball from above the head.

Plate 26 Alan Williams uses timing to get up first for his height shot, thus allowing himself a lower release from a forward position.

Plate 27 a and b Paul Patterson just before, and Rich Pearce just after, the release in a long range height shot.

the ball is thrust downwards from directly above the ring (Dunk Shot).

As the shooter moves further away from the basket, he develops more release force either by shooting from a bent arm position, or by releasing the ball on his way up the jump, or both. These mean that the ball is released at a lower point, until with shots from 25–35 feet the ball may be released just as the feet leave the floor on the jump. The actual degree of elbow force and jumping force imparted to the ball depends upon the skill and touch of the shooter. Some can shoot effortless height shots from the top of a jump at 20 feet, using bent arm techniques.

There are many trusting souls in basketball who believe that a player can 'hang' in the air while performing a height shot. This is, of course, an illusion created by players who can jump very high and so spend a much longer time in the air, or by players causing their upper body to remain relatively stationary by moving the lower body very quickly in the direction the whole body is moving. That is, just before reaching the top of his jump the player lifts his legs violently up behind him, having the effect of stopping the upwards movement of the upper body. After a short time, when the body is beginning its downwards movement, the legs are again lowered quickly, with the effect that the upper body remains relatively stationary. The overall effect is that the upper body remains stationary for a short period of time, but never reaches as high a position as it would normally do during such a jump. On the whole the losses seem greater than the gains, and the practice is not to be widely recommended.

During jumping shots there is a certain amount of time when the ball is at risk, that is, when it is within reach of the defender. Normal protective precautions of shielding and moving the ball should be taken during all phases until the

Plate 28
Thomas using a fadeaway shot to gain a height advantage.

47

height advantage has been established. The actual release position can also be altered to counter the position of a defender's hand; it is not obligatory for the ball to be released in front of and/or directly above the head! However, it must be remembered that the off line shooting angle poses an extra problem.

One last consideration about jumping shots is that the jump need not necessarily be vertically upwards. When taken on the run, or when moving away from a defender, lateral movement can be especially effective—though it makes the aiming calculations more difficult (page 28). A common jumping shot is when the shooter who has a defender between him and basket, jumps backwards and upwards to establish a height difference. This is called a Fadeaway Shot (Plate 28). However, since the force developed by the legs and trunk is away from basket, unusually efficient use of arms must be made to counteract this force. The shot cannot be made over anything other than medium or short ranges.

Obstruction Shots

These shots use part of the shooter's body as an obstruction to prevent the defender reaching the ball. The category is even less definitive than others because it is only a small minority of shots that are made purely on obstruction principles. However, those principles exist, and should be considered.

We have already seen (page 25) that the ball can be shielded by the body so that a defender cannot touch it. If sufficient force could be given to the ball in that position for a shot to be made, then the shot would be unstoppable. Obstruction shots, therefore, tend to be made from the defensive working position, and to maintain the relative positions of ball, body and defender. During the early part of the shot, the arms may be straight or bent, and are lifted, giving force to the ball. At the same time the body is turned slightly, to make it possible for the shooter to turn his head and see the basket or backboard. At any time after passing shoulder height the ball can be released from one or two hands. The majority tend to be one handed shots to maintain the defensive distance, especially

Plate 29 Carl Olson with a good long range hook shot.

Plate 30 Malcolm Campbell at the end of a very effective turnaround shot. Stopping the shot was so difficult that his defender did not make an attempt.

with a straight arm (called Hook Shots). Others, which use a bent arm but which are more easily checked are called Turnaround Shots.

The later the ball is released, the easier it is to check, and such shots tend to be combined with a movement away from the defender, or a jump, or both.

One particular shot which should be mentioned is used when an attacker has gained an inside edge *en route* to basket. The defender is so close as to make a shot difficult, so that the shooter has to protect his normal shot by using the arm furthest from the defender to release the ball, with the other arm raised as an obstruction. Because the shot was made possible by penetration, and released from a height, it is impossible to categorise. In the modern game it is so often used

49

in its many variations, mainly because of its combination of good shooting principles, yet it does not have a name of its own. It is hardly a lay up, which denotes a rather easy path to basket—not a hook shot, even though it may use a hooking action—not a jump shot, even though taken from a jump. I think that it should be called a Drive Shot, because it takes determination and drive to perform it, and it normally comes at the end of a drive towards basket.

Plate 31 a, b and c Thomas with three similar drives which release the ball from higher or lower, behind or in front of the board, left or right foot take off etc., etc.

Free Shots

In the modern game, the only shots which fall completely into this category are penalty shots, where an absolutely free attempt to score is allowed from a certain area on court. But one should also consider the implications of this type of shooting in two other sets of circumstances. One, where a shot is taken from outside the area of court which is being defended; or defenders are prevented from reaching the shooter by a physical obstacle (a Block), or by a lack of time. Two, where the shooter has received the ball well ahead of the defence (a Stealaway) and has free access to the basket, with plenty of time for the shot.

Since these shots are not opposed, the circumstances in which they are taken are very similar from one time to another.

The foul shot is, of course, the best example of unchanging circumstances; but the Set Shot taken from long distance can be performed in such a way that it is usually taken from approximately the same floor position, or from the same distance on an arc around the basket; also the free Lay Up Shot tends to be taken in a similar fashion on each occasion—so much so that a player will often take a longer path to basket just to ensure that his final approach angle and speed are what he is accustomed to.

Skills which tend to be performed in the same manner on every occasion are called Closed Skills. Because of their repetitive nature, the training and match performance tends to be grooved in a certain pattern, and to be relatively less liable to error than other skills. For instance, the shooting percentage of the very best players in the world tends to be about 60 per cent with close to basket shots. Yet from the free throw line the best percentages are well up into the 80s.

A grooved pattern, then, is what must be developed in free shooting. This has obvious implications in training, which are not our immediate concern, but during the game players must realise how essential it is that their feet are always positioned on the same spot (whether running or standing)—that their angle to the basket, their grip on the ball, the speed of the movement etc. are always the same. Then they may expect greatest accuracy in their shooting.

Foul Shot

A player is entitled to assume that the conditions are almost precisely the same for all his foul shots, particularly the height, distance and size of the ring. The ball's characteristics are not so precisely controlled, but are still within a small tolerance range. A player should therefore carefully select his stance behind the line, and then look at the ring to ensure that he is facing in exactly the right direction. He is then ready to start his throw, and should accept the ball from the referee. From that time onwards, he is a machine, running through his predetermined pattern, irrespective of what technique he uses. Within limits, it should not matter what happens to his environment from then on. The crowd may shout—he should

Plate 32 a and b Two consecutive foul shots from Mags Moeran, (a) being slightly in advance of (b). Note the similarity.

be deaf. The lights may fade—he should be blind. He is an automaton. In fact, many experiments have shown that if a good foul shooter is deprived of light just before releasing the ball, it has no significant effect on his percentage of scored shots.

In order to funnel themselves into this grooved pathway, many players go through a preliminary ritual—maybe bouncing the ball a couple of times, or taking a deep breath—just before the shot itself. The body seems to recognise this series of actions and to accept it as a trigger to set off the automatic movements to come.

There are many techniques of foul shooting used by top players throughout the world, and it does seem as if the specific technique used is relatively unimportant. The basic principles of throwing still apply, and provided one adheres to those, the rest does not seem to matter. One or two points should be borne in mind, though. Since training time is never as extensive as one might wish, it is possible that by using an action for the foul shot which is similar to an action used in other shots, training on one shot will at the same time benefit others. Extensive research on this 'transfer of training' effect has still not clarified the situation, but my subjective opinion is that there *is* value in using similar techniques for the different situations.

Another theory of mine, not based upon experimental evidence but which has proved very successful for many players in my own environment, is that by cutting movements down to a minimum, one also reduces the possible sources of error. The player must discover how few joints he needs to move in order to make sufficiently high arch foul shot, and develop his ability to shoot just using those joints. In most cases this involves the shooter standing upright, with the ball held in one or two hands just above the head, with elbows and wrists bent. Without moving anything from the shoulders downwards, the arms and hands extend vigorously in the direction the ball must fly. The shot is normally direct into the ring, without using the backboard. A transfer of training effect is gained, if one handed—towards touch in jump shooting, if two handed—towards efficiency in a longer range two hands shot.

Set Shot

To be a free shot, a set shot needs to be taken at considerable range from the basket, usually somewhere between 25 and 40 feet out. From such ranges it is obvious that shooters cannot expect very high percentages, but there are players who can approach 40 per cent success, and there are many occasions when a team finds it desirable to use such shooting as a part of its tactical offence.

The power needed to throw a ball that far, particularly

Plate 33 a and b Bill Worth just leaving the floor and just after releasing the ball on a one handed set shot. He releases from a fairly high hand position whereas other players may release from further in front of the body.

since such a high trajectory is needed, is considerable, and demands a great contribution from the lower body. In many cases players also find it advisable to move forwards during the shot, from a single step or a short run. Two handed techniques are normally used, either from the middle working position, or from an overhead position. However, since the distance from the basket is so great, the off line angle is minimised and one hand shooting from the shoulder can be used with success. In the early 1960's Hungary won quite a few tight ball games by giving Greminger the ball just inside the front court with a few seconds to the end of the game. He was so confident of his one hand from the shoulder shot from that distance, that inevitably it went in!

Since there is such a strong leg involvement in this shot, players will often leave the floor, making it a jump shot with an early release of the ball. My own preference was for a one handed set shot (from a jump) taken from the front edge of the centre circle. Defences were always taken by surprise, so that it was a free shot and it was very often preferable to shoot 40 per cent from there than to risk getting clobbered and shoot 35 per cent from closer in!

Lay Up Shot

In this case, I draw a distinction between the free lay up shot and the drive shot mentioned on page 40. The shooter tries to perform a lay up as closed skill, which is neither desirable nor reliable in an opposed driving situation.

The approach to the basket is generally at a speed which, though it may vary early on, is brought to a predetermined rate during the last few strides. Similarly, whatever the initial line taken down court, the last strides are designed to produce a constant approach angle—most players preferring about 45° to 60°, and from the dominant side.

The ball is picked up, either from a pass or a dribble, at a point which allows the shooter to perform two steps before arriving at the basket. The early approach is adjusted so that these two steps are Right–Left in the case of a right handed shot (and vice versa). During these steps the shooter begins to lose his forward lean, as he wishes to convert some of his forward momentum upwards, and the last step is taken with the foot well forward with the free leg starting to drive upwards at the same time as the ball is lifted upwards in two hands.

Since the idea of the jump is to gain height, the arms are also stretched upwards, the ball being carried to the greatest possible height with the shooting hand either underneath or behind the ball and the other hand supporting it from the side or underneath. When the ball is but a few inches from the board it is pushed softly, with a small degree of spin, on to the board at a predetermined spot, so that it drops easily into the

55

Plate 34 Free lay up shot by Thomas. Note the similarity with many drive shots, though the author prefers 'underhand' shots in most circumstances. The ball is released very close to the board.

ring. If the shooting hand is behind the ball, the spin is back-spin. When the shooting hand is underneath, if any spin is used it is normally sidespin.

I make no apology for having described the lay up shot so precisely, since it is a relatively closed skill in a free situation. However, I must reiterate that the drive situation is completely different, and that though *some* drive shots may be very similar to lay up shots, it is the differences between them that allow the shooter to beat his defender. During training, the good coach will emphasise this difference in outlook between free and opposed shots—and nowhere is it more necessary than in 'lay up' versus 'drive'!

BOUNCING

With this fundamental we are basically concerned with the techniques of dribbling, though the principles also apply to bounce passing. In many basketball environments, dribbling is regarded in rather bad odour—the word being synonymous with selfishness and greed. To me, this is as illogical as saying that shooting is selfish, or even that checking shots is greedy. In all team efforts, the attempt should be made to get the best people for a given job to *do* that job. The best shooter should do most of the shooting, the best passer do most of the passing, and the best dribbler do most of the dribbling. To say that any one skill is less desirable or important than any other is dangerous in that it encourages the development of an unbalanced team, or player. Dribbling is a part of basketball, it should therefore be performed well.

Inasmuch as bouncing the ball involves throwing it and catching it, many of the principles of control have been covered in previous sections (pages 15 and 26). But dribbling has certain restrictions imposed upon it by the rules, which necessitate a modification in the application of these principles. Some of the rules are very explicit, for instance that only a single hand should be used on each bounce. Some are far less explicit, particularly the 'palming' or carrying rules. What would be acceptable and skilful dribbling in one league, or country, would be illegal 'palming' in another.

Basically there are two forms of dribbling. One, where the dribble is unopposed, and the only consideration is to make ground (perhaps quickly). Two, where the dribble is opposed and the ball must be protected, even though the dribbler may be moving quickly or attacking the basket strongly.

Unopposed Dribble

In the case where the dribbler is moving very little or not at all it doesn't much matter how he dribbles, he is just killing time and his control of the ball does not need to be more than minimal. If, however, he is moving quickly or very quickly he needs to pay much more attention to his control of the ball. In order to move quickly over a long distance, the dribbler needs an upright stance, which imposes a lower limit below which he cannot contact the ball—this being at about hip height. Since running fast demands smooth co-ordination of limbs, the fewer 'non running' movements made with the arms the better. Therefore the 'stride to bounce ratio' should be high, such a situation being achieved by higher bounces. If the bounce is too high it becomes more difficult to control on the run, because the arms have to be carried too high. The happy medium for such dribbling seems to be at about waist height.

The easiest place to see and reach a ball is in front of the body, so the bounce on an unopposed dribble is in front and slightly to one side of the body (to avoid the feet). The dribbler is, therefore, running onto the ball, which is much safer than running away from it as would be the case in a side or rear dribble.

Plate 35 Chicks number 42 reaches down for the ball to catch it early with his fingertips.

The relative infrequency of bounces means that the hand also contacts the ball infrequently, making control more difficult. The tendency, then, should be for the dribbler to catch the ball early in its upward flight—to maintain contact with it over the top of its flight path—and then to push it downwards to the next bounce. Most referees will accept that contact with the ball must occupy *some* period of time, and the usual criterion of the legality of this contact is the extent to which the direction the ball is moving is changed by this contact, especially if it is associated with a rolling action of hand and wrist.

Plate 36 Thomas, having firmly established the catch, ball at hip height, and to one side of the body.

The safest method of achieving this contact is to ensure that the catch is performed with the hand and wrist directly in line with and behind the rising ball. If the hand is inclined downwards, the first contact is with the fingertips (spread) which give with the ball until maximum contact is established with fingers *and* palm. This process involves a flexion of the wrist which, combined with elbow flexion, takes the ball up to the top of its flight. The hand should then be on the ball *directly behind* the proposed line of thrust (Fig. 12).

59

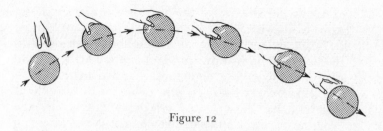

Figure 12

The push is almost directly downwards as far as the arm is concerned, the ball's forward motion being caused by the total movement of the body. But since the resultant force on the ball is forwards and downwards, the wrist remains cocked during the majority of the push, the ball then rolling off the fingertips. This action automatically puts 'back spin' on the ball, having the effect of making the ball rise more sharply—and being more easily caught.

Plate 37 Bill Worth, having begun the throw from waist height.

Plate 38 John Siddall just at the release, the position of the fingertips showing that back spin must have been applied to the ball.

Plate 39 Bill Worth after the release, with the ball well in front of the body at high speed.

Many players dribble with the ball more to the side, which means that the forearm is positioned laterally to the direction of the ball. The tendency is then for the hand to roll over the ball, which is not only less effective, but more likely to be judged illegal.

Protective Dribble

This technique must be used when a defender is threatening the ball, the presumption being that he is making movements of his hand towards the ball, or is maintaining a position which prevents the ball going in a given direction. In either case, the dribbler needs greater control of the ball and an increased ability to change the direction of the ball quickly. These two requirements are met by dribbling lower down, so that the hand can be in contact with the ball for a proportionately greater period of time, and more bounces are made per unit time. The force applied to the ball is greater than in a high dribble, and the wrist and finger action is much firmer, with less (or no) contact between the palm and the ball.

Plate 40 Thomas maintaining protection and control with a low bounce.

Following the basic principle that the hand must be directly behind and in line with the proposed direction of the ball, the increased mobility of the protective dribble is achieved by turning the arm and wrist quickly while the ball bounces, and also by varying the pressure exerted by different fingers. It is vital that the turn is achieved *between* contacts rather than *during* contact if 'palming' violations are to be avoided. Players who do not have unusually long arms and unusually

Plate 41 a, b and c Bill Worth and Thomas showing three typical phases during change of direction. Note the hand is always *behind* the proposed line of flight, and changing dribbling hand is the easiest way to change direction without 'palming' the ball.

short legs will find it necessary to crouch in order to dribble low, such a stance being a ball protection in itself if the body is between the ball and defender. It is essential with the protective dribble, and advisable with the unopposed dribble, that the dribbler focusses his vision elsewhere than on the ball. It may still be seen on the periphery of the visual field, but the dribbler should not need to see the ball directly in order to maintain control, his main need being to be aware of the

63

Plate 42 Thomas looking away while dribbling.

situation around him. Certainly at elementary level, looking at the ball ranks with 'one handedness' as a cardinal sin.

May I finish by making a plea that dribbling should not become a neglected art. Young players take a delight in acquiring ball control, and the judicious practice of dribbling can prove attractive to boys and help to develop them as 'complete' basketballers.

HITTING

The term 'hitting' is used in opposition to 'catching and throwing', to describe those actions where, rather than the body absorbing the ball's force, the ball absorbs the body's force. The ball is in fact struck, to cause it to change direction and/or speed. The main occasions when it happens are during jump balls and rebounding situations. Here, the player contacting the ball has very little room to manoeuvre, maybe only an inch advantage at the top of a jump (Fig. 13).

He can hit the ball without his opponent being able to touch it, but he cannot catch the ball without allowing his opponent an opportunity of interfering with the catch.

64

Plate 43 Bill Worth and Bill Robson showing the fingertip involvement during a close tip off.

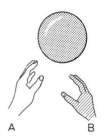 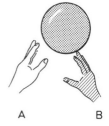

A   B   A   B

Figure 13

Since the ball must rebound from the fingertips, it is essential that the whole upper limb be like a steel spring, under tension and with an absence of 'softness'. The ball can only rebound if there is force between it and the fingertips. In some cases, where the ball is moving fairly fast, then it provides its own force; but on many occasions the ball is near the top of its flight and has very little movement. Then, the arm must be moving in the general direction which the ball is required to go, and the movement accelerated with a sharp wrist flexion at the moment of contact.

65

C

Plate 44 Alan Williams has his wrist flexed, ready to snap the hands forwards to hit the ball on the tip.

Plate 45 Excellent tipping technique robs a taller player of the ball.

If the height advantage has been gained in a 'relative' way (page 44) then the ball could be contacted at any point during the jump, and even held momentarily on straight fingers. In this case player and opponent could be moving together up and down on a jump with the same height difference existing between them at all times. This action, though more rigid than others, is not a hit, and the force to propel needs to be developed in other ways.

The direction in which the ball can be hit depends entirely upon the proximity of opponents' hands. If they are sufficiently low, then the ball can be hit sideways or downwards, e.g. hitting a ball which is on the ring into basket, hitting an upwards rising rebound straight back down through the ring, hitting a rebound or jump ball straight down to a team mate. If opponents' hands are too high to permit such movements, then the fingers of the hitting hand(s) must be turned slightly upwards and the ball lobbed over the obstruction. This action should also be used on a Tip In Shot made from a rebound below the ring, the ball being hit preferably onto the board to rebound into the ring, but can be hit direct into the ring.

Plate 46 Carl Sylvester lobbing the ball over an opponent.
Plate 47 Alan Williams beginning a bent arm Tip In shot.

In general, such shots are made one handed, because the very proximity of defenders which makes a hit necessary also makes a one handed stretch more effective. In some cases, though, two hands may be possible, providing a very great improvement in accuracy.

Hitting actions may also be used in deflecting high passes, but the action involves a very high skill level—not only that the pass may be accurate, but also that injury to the fingers may be avoided. Much highly specific practice is necessary in order to develop this ability, but it is practice that can reap big dividends in terms of possessions gained and tip in shots scored.

MOVING

Most movement in basketball is done without the ball, and for that reason the only body movements we have really examined so far have been those directly concerned with the ball. Basic positions and movements of the body are used irrespective of the player having the ball or not, and we shall now examine these in greater detail.

A player can only move himself by exerting force, in almost all cases against the floor, though he may occasionally push himself off another player. The efficiency with which he moves

Plate 48 Jim Anatol pushes off Gary Brown to move higher on a jump.

depends, then, upon his technique of contacting the floor, and the extent of friction (grip) between his shoes and the floor. This statement holds good even if the movement is restricted to body parts other than the feet—which still act as base for the movement. I shall assume in the following paragraphs that players have virtually perfect grip with the floor, assuming also that any player who is sufficiently interested in his personal development to read this book must have taken the elementary step of providing himself with the best footwear obtainable!

Lateral Movement

The stance adopted by a player will depend entirely on the probability of his moving in any particular direction. If we consider lateral movement around the court first, a player could *theoretically* move in any direction. He can also *practically* move in any direction, but will find it easier to move in some directions than others. By adopting the best stance for any given direction, then *that* movement will be the easiest for him to perform.

The reasons for this are not difficult to understand. We have seen earlier how a force has greatest effect if it is applied behind and exactly in line with the required direction of movement. While this is possible with a ball (Fig. 14), it is not possible with the body (Fig. 15).

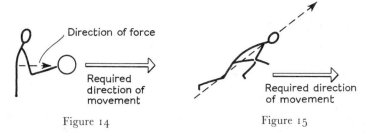

Figure 14   Figure 15

However far a runner leans forward, he can never achieve a perfect thrusting position, so that in fact only a part of his force is being used to propel him laterally. The rest goes in overcoming the effects of other forces, particularly gravity.

Within the limits of a player's mobility and power, a pronounced body lean in the required direction of movement will help him to start quickly and achieve greatest speed. But basketball is a game of deception, and quick changes of direction, so that a body lean position which is very good for moving in one direction is no good at all for moving in a substantially different path. Players have to choose a stance which can be easily adapted to any one of several directions,

Plate 49 Alan Williams shows pronounced body lean in starting quickly for a rebound.

Plate 50 Pronounced body lean and flat driving foot position at the start of a drive by Thomas.

Plate 51 Examples of body lean by 8 stopping, 10 changing direction and 14 running.

being helped in the knowledge that defenders usually have to move sideways or backwards, with attackers mainly moving sideways and forwards.

If we look at a player with a wide foot position (Fig. 16), we can see that merely by lifting a foot he puts himself in a good position to push with the other foot.

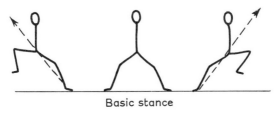

Basic stance

Figure 16

This position should be a comfortable one, if it is strained then muscles cannot work as efficiently. The mobility and power of a player's hips and legs are of great importance in the achievement of his basic stance, but an exaggerated low stance has other implications for players who need a certain amount of height, which might mean a further modification in the position.

To return to Figure 16, we can see that if our pin man is facing us, then the directions in which he can move best are sideways. If, however, we consider him as being sideways on to us, then his best directions are forwards or backwards. The player's foot position is also important in the subsidiary movements, so that if we look at the plan view shown in Figure 17, we can get an idea of the relative ease with which a player may move in any lateral direction.

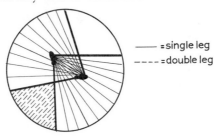

——— = single leg
– – – – = double leg

Figure 17

All joints which are used to produce movement need to be in a 'cocked' position, from which the joint extends (or flexes) and produces force. The final transmission of force to the floor is achieved by extension of the ankle(s), therefore before the push can take place the ankle must be cocked— which puts the heel on the floor. Movements which must be done speedily should not involve gross preparatory movements—so the position which allows basketballers to thrust most quickly is a *flatfooted* one. The general admonition to 'Keep on your toes' may have useful significance in describing one's concentration, but is merely a tiring method of slowing down one's physical reactions if taken literally!

Plate 52 Seven players moving—each with one foot firmly flat on the floor.

This cocked position also applies to the knees and hips, and should be maintained for the major part of the game, particularly during phases of 'close combat'. A great deal of local muscle stamina is needed in the legs, and unfortunately not many players take the trouble to develop this ability. To be a 100 per cent player when on court, I believe it essential for a player to have sufficient leg endurance to maintain these mechanically advantageous stances.

Just as it takes force to start a movement, it also takes force to change the rate or direction of that movement. When a player wants to change direction he merely needs to extend a leg to the side opposite the direction in which he wants to go, and to push in the same way previously described. One

Plate 53 Thomas and opponent changing direction for a loose ball. Both have to put out a leg, foot flat, from which to push.

difficulty arises if he happens to be standing on the 'wrong' leg at the time! For instance, a player running forwards and needing suddenly to turn left is in difficulties if he happens to have his right foot already on the ground. The turn can still be achieved by bringing his left foot across the body and putting it outside the right—though this is more difficult than a normal swerve (Fig. 18).

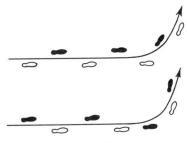

Figure 18

73

Plate 54 a and b Pete Siddall (12) and Vic Collins (10) using cross step swerves to avoid being wrong footed.

When performing sharp turns players should bend their knees more, thus lowering the body to make the direction of thrust nearer to the horizontal.

For the same reason, bodyweight should be kept low when stopping, with a reverse force being applied by putting one or both feet well in advance of the body. If one foot is used, the action is just like an extra long stride (Stride Stop), putting the body in a well balanced stance. If two feet are used, the last step is more like a long low jump, bringing the player into a less balanced position, but allowing him the facility of pivotting on either foot if he is holding the ball. As the legs

74

Plate 55 Stride stop by 15.

bend to absorb the force of the movement, they store energy within the natural elasticity of the muscles, which puts them in good position both mechanically and physiologically to immediately produce a new force, and a new movement—either straight up into a jump, or off in a new direction.

Vertical Movement

Though the same principles of force application apply in the case of jumping, the concept of relative height affects the way in which these principles are applied.

We must consider two situations; one where the jumper has plenty of time in which to make his jump, and is interested mainly in achieving absolute height (eg. during a jump ball or high rebound)—two, where he has little time in which to jump, and wants merely to be higher than his opponent (eg. during a quick jump shot, or an inconclusive tipping situation). In the first case, the jumper will extensively flex his leg joints, crouching fairly deep, perhaps after stepping into the jumping position to develop early momentum. He will then thrust upwards, swinging both arms high at the same time, and maybe tilt one shoulder upwards to reach higher with a single hand. If the jump is made from one leg because it takes place

75

Plate 56 Thomas moving into the starting position for a rebound jump.

Plate 57 Players ending a rebound jump with two arms high, by comparison with plate 48 where all have used one arm and tilted shoulders.

from a run or single step approach, the free leg is bent at the knee and also driven upwards as if tied to the arms during the jump.

In the second case there is not sufficient time for an extensive flexing of the leg joints. If taken from a standing position, the arms may be already raised to shoulder height or above, and a vigorous extension of the ankles is the main source of power with perhaps just a slight flexing of the knees (Plate 58). If the jump is made from a run, or immediately following another jump, the momentum of the body is merely converted into an upwards direction by the player literally bouncing off rigid legs, using only the balls of his feet, with the heels raised and a very slight flexion of knees and ankles. This movement requires specialised training, but it is certainly the fastest way of getting airborne, and very necessary in tight situations.

During two foot take-offs, a wide stance is not necessary, since no lateral force is required. The closer the feet are together, the higher the body is at the beginning (and top) of the jump. Depending upon the balance of the player, and the

76

Plate 58 Quick jumping stance for relative height, shown by Colin Smith waiting for a forward tip from Carl Sylvester (14).

stability of the situation, the feet therefore are kept only a matter of inches apart.

Arm Movements

The arms, being relatively weak, need two different techniques in the production of movement. There are instances when the arms need to develop great speed in the ball, particularly on long passes. Keeping the arm straight whilst swinging at the shoulder joint ensures that the ball, being on the furthest circumference of the circle, is moving at its fastest. This uses the arm as a long lever.

But on most occasions, the arms need to be moved quickly in themselves, the whole mass of the arms—not just the ends. Here, a shorter lever system is better, with the arms well bent at the elbow. The greater leverage of such positions is also useful in ball holding, enabling the holder to push or pull the ball through any defensive attempts to capture it.

Fake Movements

In order to deceive opponents, players will often pretend to be making a movement which they do not intend to complete. The fake is most deceptive when it most closely resembles the actual movement, in fact, when it *is* the movement. If the movement is such that it can be stopped or changed quite easily, then there are no problems—for instance, a player can fake a two hand pass, and merely hold on to the ball instead of releasing it. The fake can be an exact copy.

But some movements cannot be easily stopped. For instance, if the movements which produce a jump are exactly performed, then the player will leave the floor—he cannot stop himself. These movements are very difficult to fake, and can only be done successfully by creating an illusion. In the jumping fake, if the player starts from a straight leg crouch, by lifting his head, trunk, arms and ball upwards *at the same time as* bending his knees and ankles, the two movements can cancel one another creating no jumping force, and yet giving a very good illusion of take off.

Fakes must be either real or realistic—coaches and players must know the difference between them in different situations, if they are to develop the most effective methods.

SPACE

A basketball court is, to all intents and purposes, just a big open-sided box, in which are two goals and a lot of space. Into this space come ten players, two officials and a ball. The players try to make the best use of this space in three ways; one by causing their opponents to occupy certain spaces, and two, by filling other spaces themselves. The third use of space is, of course, by limiting the ball to specific positions and movements.

The ball is essentially the free-est item filling a space. It can fly faster and higher (and even further laterally) than a man, but is incapable of producing this movement itself. The ball, then, must always be associated with one or more players. Another important difference between ball and man as 'space fillers', is that the ball is very much smaller than the man, and can therefore penetrate more easily into confined spaces.

The player, though more restricted in the extent and speed of his movements, has two main advantages over the ball. He can change direction laterally during a movement to a much greater extent than the ball, and he can initiate his own movement.

If we now examine some of the things that we have said ball and/or man are required to do during the game, we can get an idea of how to do them in terms of occupying and moving through space.

Information (page 18): It is easier to see a man than the ball. When planning signals to which players respond, especially in complex moving situations, the movement of a man is more likely to be appreciated than the movement of the ball.

Force (page 26): The application of force is made most powerfully by a player. The ball *can* apply force, using the energy it possesses by virtue of its own movement, but that force is originally provided by the player, who must always be capable of developing even more force. If, therefore, a situation develops which needs force to overcome it (such as closely opposed shot), the passage of ball and/or man *through* the opposed space is best made by the player. If contact is necessary to impart force against the obstacle (a defender), then it could be made by the body (where legal or acceptable) or by the ball held firmly in the hands.

Mobility (page 34): Because of his intrinsic ability to change direction, mobility within space is best achieved by the player. But one should remember that the ball can have extrinsic mobility when under the control of one or more players—by close interpassing, dribbling, or defensive holding.

Penetration (page 39): When the space to be penetrated is a small one, it may be that only a ball could get through it. So the ball may have to be thrown through the space. If it is required that the ball change direction *after* penetrating the space, then it must be held during the penetration so at least an arm must accompany it through the gap.

Height (page 44): *Eventually*, height is best achieved by the ball, though the player's control of the ball may be maintained for as long (high) as possible before release. This height may be used, of course, for passing and shooting.

Obstruction (page 48): By definition, obstruction is provided by the body, or part of the body. However, in some close to basket work the obstruction can be provided by the ring, net or backboard.

Free Space (page 50): This is the ideal situation at which all play should aim. The creation of space which is free from opposition is, therefore, uppermost in all coaches' minds, and the latter part of this book is devoted to the theme in some detail.

Moving: In absolute terms, the ball can move faster than a player, but such movement is useful *only* if there is someone to receive the ball who is in a better offensive position, or if tactical manoeuvres are being made. In the relative sense, space can be traversed quicker by a player dribbling the ball, than by players running in the same direction passing the ball. Not only is it quicker, but safer in terms of freedom from error. Figure 19 shows an experiment which will demonstrate this fact to those who might not be disposed to believe it.

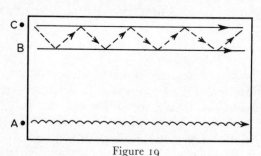

Figure 19

If A, B and C all start at the same time, given equal ability and effort, A will reach the other end first.

It is as well to remember that space extends in all directions. Many players make inefficient use of space, or rather, *insufficient* use of the space around them. It may seem trite to make the point that movements *can* be made forwards, back-wards, sideways and obliquely—upwards and downwards. But many players are restricted by a lack of mobility, skill, power and physique, from using all the available space. Such players are easier to oppose than the 'allround' mover!

PATTERNS

So far in our consideration of basketball fundamentals we have been concerned mainly with the individual and the ball, occasionally also his defender. Now we must extend the scope of fundamentals to include the interaction of groups of players within the space available to them. At any stage of play, the ten players will be in a certain position relative to one another, the ball *and* the court. Call this the 'pattern'—offensive pattern for the team with the ball, and defensive pattern for their opponents.

At this stage we must really define the various categories of pattern which exist, leaving comment on the deeper tactical implications to a later section of the book. The most common international convention is to describe patterns in terms of the numbers of players contained in each lateral rank, starting from the centre of the court and going towards the endline (Fig. 20).

This convention applies to both offensive and defensive patterns, but makes no differentiation between the various positions of the ranks relative to the court, and is not specific regarding each player's position along his rank. There does not appear to be a general convention to describe other aspects of pattern, so that I must now propose my own terms, within which framework I can at least make the remainder of this book more understandable. Before looking at team patterns, we must first define positions (and functions) taken by individual players.

Guard: A player who mainly occupies that part of the pattern which is furthest away from the endline concerned. If he is the organising genius in setting up the offence, he may be called a 'Quarter-back'—a term borrowed from American football.

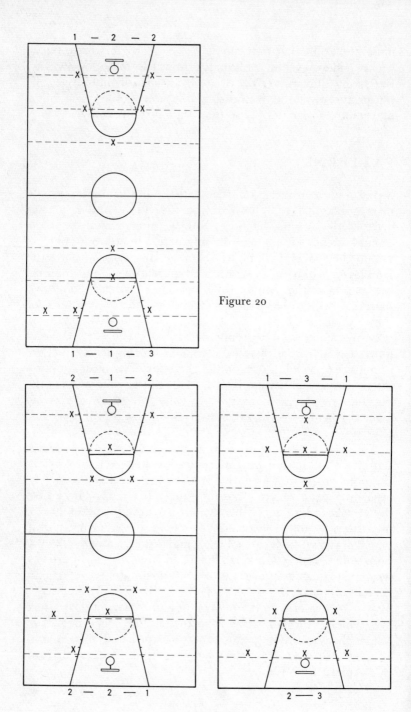

Figure 20

Forward: A player who mainly occupies that part of the pattern which is nearest the endline concerned—though he still may be as far out as the free throw line.

Centre: A player who mainly moves in the area close to the basket concerned. He is popularly also called 'Pivot' and 'Post' depending on his specific function, and whether on offence or defence. This superfluity of terms causes great confusion in communication, throughout the whole world. So, I propose just to use the word 'Centre'.

These three are the basic positional definitions, though the playing systems being used may make it difficult to be absolutely water tight. For example, there are occasions when a team might play 1–3–1 offence and 2–1–2 defence. There will then be one guard, two forwards, and two centres on offence—with two guards, two forwards and one centre on defence. So, one player is a guard/forward, and another is a forward/centre (I exclude the remote possibility of a player being sufficiently talented to be a guard/centre—though it used to happen a great deal in the 1940's, and still does in some extremely specialised tactics). Figure 21 should make the position clear, though this is not the only pattern to suit our particular example.

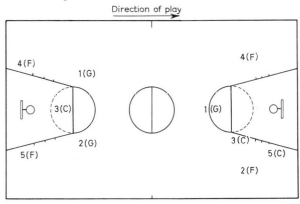

Figure 21

Another anomalous situation arises in the case of a 1–2–2 defence, where these definitions become a little stretched. However, if one merely reverses the same offensive pattern, it seems rational to retain the positional terms (Fig. 22).

83

The discerning reader will by now have noticed that there tend to be two types of pattern. One, where there is a Centre surrounded by other players; two, where there is no such centre. I define these as Closed and Open patterns.

Closed

These are patterns having a Centre and of the 1–3–1, 2–3 and 2–1–2 variety (Fig. 23).

In such patterns, the Centre is 'next in line' to each of the other four players, thus providing a more tightly knit formation on both offence and defence.

Open

Such patterns are often called 'Horseshoe' and are of the form seen in Figure 24 (1–2–2), (2–2–1) and (2–1–2).

Play tends to be spread over a wide area—mainly on the perimeter, with individual forays being made into the centre and towards the basket.

Some offensive patterns tend to concentrate a high proportion of players (three or more) in one area of court—generally on one side of the key or other. This causes an 'Overload', and generally seeks to outnumber the defence. (Examples: Fig. 23 a, Fig. 24 b and c.)

Moving Patterns

Our consideration so far has been of patterns which are maintained in a relatively stationary way, or of particular formations through which a team might pass during a total team movement. Such patterns are useful as a starting point, or a key point during movement, from which specific action will take place. This action might be formally proscribed (a Set Play), or be devised on the spot by the players' reactions to the situation (Free Play).

Any movement which then takes place can be considered basically as it affects any two players. Figure 25 shows these effects, subdivided into four distinct classifications, with a few examples of these.

Direction of play

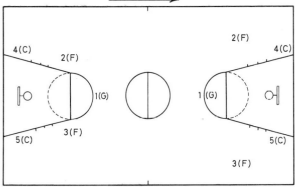

Figure 22

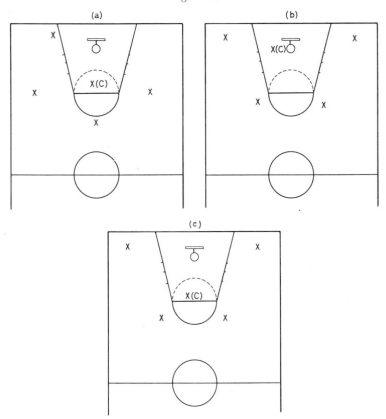

Figure 23

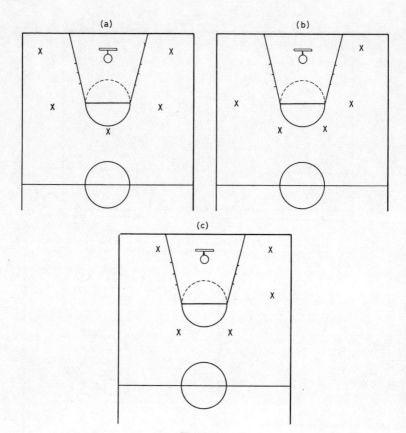

Figure 24

Figure 25

In general, Convergent movement requires the distance between two players to be decreasing, Divergence means the distance is increasing, Radial that one player is moving around the other at a fairly constant distance, and Parallel movement requires the two to be moving in about the same direction at about the same speed and remaining approximately the same distance apart.

Naturally, almost all *team* movements will involve more than one of these four, even if one only considers that there are ten pairs in a team of five. So, a player may be diverging from one team mate, whilst converging with another and running parallel to a third. In offence, then, the use of the terms is restricted to the actual movement which permits the aim of the offence to be achieved—whether that be a shot, a rebound, a pass or even a stall. In defence, movements are to a certain extent dictated by the offence, and the terms are used to describe those actual movements which oppose the critical offensive manoeuvres. In any situation involving gross team movements one may still have complex tactics such as two players converging, while another two diverge and the fifth runs parallel with one of the others. An efficient unravelling of these complicated patterns depends upon an understanding of the elements within the pattern, and the aims of the critical moves.

SUPPORT

The ideal basketball team is one which any of the players is better than any of the opposition. As a coach, I cannot remember a premier game in which I was able to say 'My worst player is better than your best player', though I can remember occasions on which the reverse was the case! In almost all cases, a coach can plan his tactics so that he has at least one of his players being opposed by an inferior opponent (or no opponent at all) on offence—and, in many cases, each of his players facing an inferior opponent on defence. The defensive problem is, of course, the greater one, but on the whole a coach needs to plan so that where an imbalance of player capacity occurs which is not in his favour, help can be given to the weaker man. Game tactics must provide 'Support' for players facing stronger opponents, or who are outnumbered.

Physical Support

This is the main way in which support is provided; team patterns are so arranged on both offence and defence that a player can use a team mate's physical presence to support what he is doing. Even more, a team mate can take over part (or all, in emergency) of a weaker player's function. In order to achieve this support, players must be near to one another, and the supporting player must be positioned so that he can move quickly into, or is already standing in, an area where the support will be needed. In some very well drilled teams, this function is automatic and players know that support is always present. In most teams, however, reassurance or confirmation of support should be given to the outmatched player. This can be done verbally in most cases (a sadly neglected art in British basketball), especially where the player cannot see his supporting man, but information can also be given manually or visually.

Time Support

Since there are positions and situations on court when opponents have only a limited time in which to achieve certain things, players can use that 'time barrier' to accomplish part of their function for them. This applies especially to the three second area, when a defender might quite deliberately leave himself open on one side knowing that his opponent would be liable for a three second violation if he accepted that opening. Similar techniques can be used in defending out-of-bounds plays, and during defence in the defender's front court.

Offensive players have less opportunity to use time as a support, but it is commonly used in one specific situation. That situation occurs when a team in possession of the ball have a just sufficient lead to win the game, if only they can retain possession for the maximum permitted period. This time limit on possession varies in different parts of the world, but the international regulations specify 30 seconds. In such cases, time is an essential support to offensive tactics which go under the general heading of 'Stall Offence'.

Space Support

There are certain sections of playing space which are least useful to a player, or a team. In cases where a player cannot outwit his opponent in all directions, then he should select a technique which encourages his opponent towards a weak or least useful area. To take a defensive example, Figure 26 shows a wall which a defensive player has erected around his opponent.

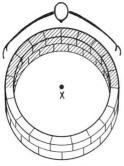

Figure 26

The shaded bricks are a physical barrier provided by the defender himself. The unshaded bricks are a mental barrier because the opponent does not wish to go in a weak or un-fruitful direction. Of course, this is 'perfect' defence, which is very rarely achieved. But it certainly can be achieved if a defender can force his opponent into a *corner* of the court, where his space support is provided by the side and end lines.

Space can also be used as defensive support by a player encouraging an opponent to use his dribble and then forcing him to stop *out of range* of the basket. Space can then form the total defence against the ball handler, leaving the defender free and perhaps giving physical support in another area.

Space is used to support offensive manoeuvres particularly in the case where a defender is outnumbered. Passes made through this space can encourage a defender to commit himself in one direction, leaving the other relatively undefended.

In summary, I should reiterate that defence poses the greater problems of under matching, and therefore the support given by space, time and physical presence is especially necessary in defensive tactics. Later, we shall encounter many specific examples of such support, and a basic understanding of support principles will make it much easier to grasp and apply the team tactics which lead towards winning games.

Part 2: Tactical applications

As generals going into battle, so players and coaches equip themselves with the weapons and manpower needed to achieve victory. The fundamental attributes I have so far discussed are these weapons, and the first job of a basketball army is to ensure that it has the necessary range of tools, that they function efficiently even under rough and dirty conditions, and that if they should break down or prove ineffective they are capable of being adapted and improvised to suit the situation.

Just as, in the last analysis, the general depends upon each individual soldier's performance, so does the game of basketball eventually rest on the shoulders of one player facing another. Excluding the often mechanical function of advancing the ball down court, the majority of the game is an interface between individual players and their opponents. So, my first consideration will be that of Individual Offence and Defence. Indeed, during the early part of my own playing career I found this such a fascinating subject that I was often quite rightly accused of caring little for the broader picture of team play! I hereby apologise to all those past team mates and coaches who suffered the 'Thomas Give and Go' tactics—that is 'Give the ball to Thomas and Go back down the other end'!

It is difficult for coaches to make their players care enough about individual play to put in the countless hours of practice necessary for individual skills—much of it done solo or with one colleague. In an interview with Bob Wilson, both Jerry West and Wilt Chamberlain admitted to 6–8 hours daily training in their formative years—and this devotion is not restricted to the American super stars. On the other hand, I know that in my own case extended personal training (about 5 hours daily) made me overconscious of individual play, especially since I had no coach around to remind me of the part I had to play in team tactics. It took many years for me to overcome this fault. I hope other players will realise early on in their careers the importance of reaching an efficient balance between individual and team play development.

INDIVIDUAL OFFENCE AND DEFENCE

I should like, at first, to analyse the general situation which exists between two opponents. One needs, in such cases, to consider offence and defence simultaneously. Special circumstances of individual play can then be covered as being departures from the general situation.

Plate 59 Quarterback calls and signals for ball at head of key. Steve Gubby ferociously protects the ball!

An attacker should try to be standing or moving in a position from which he can (and would) shoot—except for special offensive tactics such as stall plays (page 88). So let us start from such a position, for instance at the head of the key, without the ball (Fig. 27), and with the defender perhaps two or three feet away. Since we are considering only individual play, the attacker wants the ball, and the defender aims to stop him getting it. The ball, in our example, is on the left, and the defender will normally adjust his defensive stance (page 69) so that he is slightly 'Off Line' towards the ball—

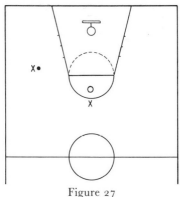
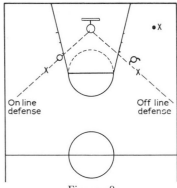

Figure 27   Figure 28

the 'line' being a direct one between attacker and basket (Fig. 28).

He then stands a good chance of intercepting any pass made to the attacker, especially if he keeps his arms flexed just outside an open passing channel. He thus encourages the pass, whilst being ready to move his arms (and body) quickly to intercept (page 77).

Having committed himself off line, the defender is now open to a cut, and the attacker can start running quickly around the back of the defender, hoping to leave him in such a stance that he cannot start quickly *and* turn. The attacker may then be able to find space in which to receive a pass, either a middle plane pass (page 35) if he has enough space, or a bounce or high plane pass (pages 36 and 38) if he is still under some pressure (Fig. 29). It may be that the defender will have turned very quickly and maintained a position between the attacker and the ball, but the attacker has still a clear penetration lane to the basket, and a high plane pass can still reach him (Fig. 30). Of course, the defender is aware of these dangers, and his original stance should be such that he can see both his man *and* the ball, in that order of importance. He does this by using peripheral vision, that is by looking along a line roughly bisecting the angle between all three, which allows him to see things at the periphery of that angle (up to about 175°). Figure 31 illustrates this technique.

So, the defender adopts a foot position which will enable him to move very quickly in the direction which the attacker

93

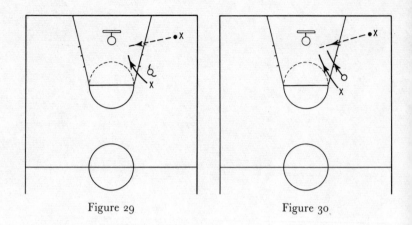

Figure 29   Figure 30

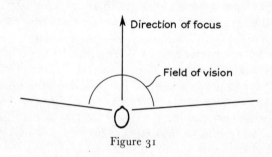

Figure 31

is likely to take. He will, of course, hope to be able to spot the attacker's intentions early enough to be able to counteract them in time. The attacker has other ideas. Unfortunately, the writer on basketball tactics tends to describe perfect tactics for perfect players—irresistible forces against immovable objects! The game is not like that; two opponents are never perfectly matched, the better man will win. And even the inferior man will attempt to reduce his deficit by playing well thus reducing the relative advantage of his opponent.

Generally, in this process of opponents reducing each other's advantage, the defender has such a responsibility to prevent the attacker from reaching a scoring position with the ball that he must overplay such a possibility. This invites the attacker to move to a less advantageous position to receive a pass. This is a cardinal defensive rule—if you must commit yourself, do so into the most dangerous area. In the situation we have been considering, the defender would therefore only commit himself to overplaying possible moves towards basket —inviting the attacker to move outwards for the ball (Fig. 32).

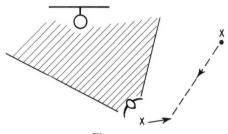

Figure 32

Faced with such a defender, the attacker should attempt to force the defender to commit himself—if possible to a weak area, but even a commitment to a dangerous area is preferable to no commitment of any type. He does this by making a manoeuvre which cannot be ignored—usually towards the basket or ball. As the defender moves back to counter the move, the attacker moves out again, leaving himself free for a pass in a weak area. Should the defender be so foolish as to move quickly back out in the realisation that the attacker had been faking, the attacker then moves straight back in again, very forcibly, and passing the defender *en route* (Fig. 33).

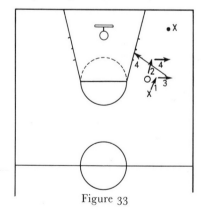

Figure 33

In this sequence, the attacker has first move (1), followed after a short interval of time by the defender (2). If the attacker is quick enough with move (3), there is a slightly longer delay before the defender makes move (4)—making it possible for the attacker to cut for the basket (4) at the same time. The defender's error has been to commit himself outwards to a less dangerous area. His particular advantage had been to be nearer the basket than the attacker, a 'distance' advantage as against the attacker's 'time' advantage. He threw his advantage away with a false move, but it could just as easily have been the attacker who made the false move, and paid for it with an interception loss and an inferior court position.

The Centre

The attacking centre and his defender have a rather unique situation. Their play takes place completely within a dangerous area, so the defender's job is to prevent his opponent getting the ball (unless he has such a tremendous defensive advantage, eg. height, as to be able to prevent his man shooting). But if the defender overplays the passing lane to the centre, he must be to a certain extent badly out of position.

Plate 60 Bill Worth (8) half fronting his man (7), though support considerations have forced him to go forward with his left side rather than his right.

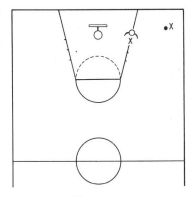
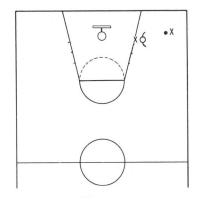

Figure 34   Figure 35

Figure 34 shows the defender 'Half Fronting' the centre, thus making reception of a pass difficult, but still allowing the defender an opportunity of getting back under the basket with his man if there should be an upper plane pass (page 38).

Figure 35 shows the defender completely 'Fronting' his man, making a direct pass virtually impossible. However, he is now very susceptible to a high plane pass, because he has to commit himself *away* from the basket. Such defence is less frequent than half fronting or in line tactics, but does use time (3 second

Plate 61 Carl Olson's (14) opponent has full fronted him, and blocked him out from a rebound.

97

area) and space for support (page 78), and is occasionally effective against a short or immobile centre.

The attacking centre will use similar tactics to free himself for a pass (page 36), handicapped by the 3 second area. In the tight and complex manoeuvres undertaken by centres there are many occasions when it becomes impossible to see both the ball and opponent. Depending upon local rule interpretations it is common practice for both attacker and defender to feel for the other's position with one hand (lightly) while focussing on the ball. This practice actually reduces the number of fouls, since opponents who are aware of each other's precise position are less liable to blunder into illegal contact.

Signalling

The player making the pass to the attacker has to decide when to release the ball, whereas in most cases the catcher knows best when and where he wants to receive it. If he can communicate this information to the thrower, then the outcome of the pass is likely to be a better one. An essential aspect, then, of getting the ball is to 'Signal' for it. At a time when the attacker knows that he is, or is about to become, free he makes a signal of some description or other. This is commonly a call or a gesture, the essence being that it should convey the information of both timing and location of the pass.

Vocal signalling uses single words or very short phrases, such as 'here', 'now', 'high', 'in', 'base line', 'behind you'— or code words which have special meaning. It has the disadvantage of being easily interpreted by the defender, who might then be able to intercept the pass, and also of being not heard in a very noisy situation. On the other hand, it can be used when the passer cannot see the man he is passing (or going to pass) to.

Gestures are usually made with the hand(s), being put firmly into the position where the ball is needed and at the time it is needed. The hands are open and in the catching position. If the catcher is going to move before getting the ball, he can point to the place he wants the ball to go—especially on high lob passes, or 'lead' passes which he will run onto while

98

Plate 62 Vic Tinsley signals for a pass, which is open because his defender has not fronted him.

driving to basket. This system of signalling is more liable to errors of reception and interpretation—but is more discreet and less likely to provoke interceptions.

Meanwhile (back at the ranch!) the defender is trying to frustrate these moves. He needs to divine the attackers' intentions. If he sees an attacker's 'Open Hand' signal, then he has to decide if it is a fake or not. If he is sure that a pass is being made, then by watching his opponent's hands or eyes he can work out when and where the ball is coming, and cut it off. The attacker may, of course, be faking and the defender must be circumspect in these moves; but the possible gains are high since not only does an interception gain possession but also gives the interceptor a space and sometimes speed advantage over his man (Fig. 36).

When a player trudges off court, slumps despondently on the bench, and complains bitterly that he is not receiving any passes—or even that he is not getting the ball in good positions —the fault is usually his own. Most players want to get the ball. Few players realise that they have to earn it by hard and intelligent offensive manoeuvring. Players mainly create their own opportunities to receive passes, and it takes considerable practice of the foregoing techniques before players can be fairly sure that they are going to get their share of lead passes.

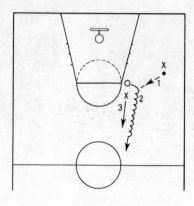

Figure 36

The joy for the defender is to deny his opponent good passes, and yet there are so few defenders who become specialists in the art. Individual defence can most easily achieve its aims if it concentrates on forcing the attacker to collect the ball where it is least useful to him. Prevention of scoring once the attacker has the ball in a dangerous area is a much more difficult proposition. The star defenders can bottle their men up and make many interceptions, usually by committing themselves wisely to a firm course of action. Occasionally, they will err, and because they are committed, the attacker will gain a very good position—maybe even score. It is too easy to forget all the other great defensive achievements of such players, and to yell caustically at them. Such lapses, provided they are very occasional, are to be expected from even the best of defenders. One must base an assessment of individual defensive efficiency on the total picture of interceptions, weak passes, lead passes and baskets a player achieves or allows.

Playing the Ball

The next phase of individual play occurs when the attacker receives the ball. There are several main categories of such situations, but the one in which the greatest scope occurs is the medium distance possession, somewhere near the middle

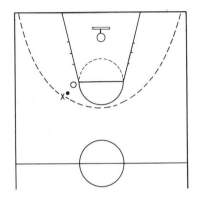

Figure 37

of an arc around 20 feet from the basket (Fig. 37). Here, the attacker has 7 basic offensive options.

1. Hold the ball
2. Pass Left
3. Pass Right
4. Pass Overhead
5. Dribble Left
6. Dribble Right
7. Shoot from the spot.

The defender has to be aware of these options, and to decide within the framework of his own team's defensive tactics which options are the most dangerous. He then defends in such a manner as to prevent the attacker from performing his strongest options, hinder his performance of medium options, but allow the performance of the weakest options.

The attacker/defender situation is very much like the conundrum of the chicken and egg. Which came first? Or rather, who decides what happens? Since the attacker has the ball, which cannot be ignored, his decision as to what to do

Plate 63 Thomas has 7 options: an immediate shot; pass, high to 11, left to 10, right to 6; drive, right of opponent (10), left of opponent (4); or hold the ball safely!

with it will determine the defensive responsibility. But, if the defender makes sufficient of the 7 options unfeasible, then he determines what moves the attacker *can* make. There is really no solution to the problem other than the commonsense one of saying that whichever of the two antagonists does his job best achieves the priority in determining what will happen in any given situation.

The early part of an encounter between two players must be devoted to discovering the main playing characteristics each uses. This analysis should, of possible, be done before the game starts by efficient 'Scouting' of the opposition at other games in which they are involved. American coaches have developed scouting into a highly complex art, especially since they have the facilities to send a scout many hundreds of miles to watch future opponents playing. Teams from other countries, particularly national teams, may also have this facility, but the majority of clubs do not, and the only foreknowledge which can be obtained by a player is based on his opponent's reputation, and perhaps his memory of previous encounters.

Assuming that the two antagonists have analysed each other's characteristics, let us now examine a few of the many hundreds of permutations of moves they might make. These will be basic and common manoeuvres which will be seen often in good class games.

1. Immediate Shot

In cases where the attacker has created space to receive a pass in a good shooting position, he may shoot as soon as he receives the ball. The defender, who has been man-oeuvred out of position, will try to recover—so the attacker does not have time to spare. If possible, he should have already begun his shooting procedure *before* receiving the ball, so that the whole action is a continuous flow of 'catch and throw'. The lateness in the movement at which it is possible to catch the ball depends mainly upon the distance the shooter is from the basket:

(a) *Long range shot.* The catch is made just at the beginning of the shot, with knees, trunk and arms bent ready to start the throw.

(b) *Medium range shot.* With height or penetration shots, the major part of force development may have started before the catch. The shooter will be moving upwards or forwards, but should make the catch with bent arms so that he still has the ability to apply force and final control to the ball. The shot is easier to perform if the ball is passed in the same general direction as the shooter is moving—but on most occasions this is hardly possible. However, one example of this point occurs when a driving player is given a bounce pass so that the ball is moving obliquely upwards when it is caught—thus helping him in his attempt to move obliquely upwards with the ball.

(c) *Close to Basket Shot.* This category may include catches made from rebounds as well as from passes. The same general considerations about reception of the ball apply,

Plate 64 A medium range immediate height shot by an unexpected receiver of the ball.

except that it can be received even later in the movement. All actions in this area tend to be very closely guarded, and centres have less time in which to control the immediate shot—however they are near the basket, which helps! Very tall centres are bound by special regulations about playing the ball when it is above 10 feet (the height of the ring). Within these regulations, the unique situation occurs where the release trajectory of the ball can be downwards, especially on immediate shots taken from a rebound (Tip In Shots). The principles of catch control mentioned on page 17 apply, but the force which propels the ball *can* be gravity—thus relieving the shooter of much of his force development problem, he merely has to stop, or 'soften' the ball's flight in a position above the ring.

Less fortunate (smaller) players who need to release the ball from below ten feet need to use the principles of release, and use a backboard, mentioned earlier (pages 42 and 44).

Immediate shots are difficult to perform, but they are also difficult to stop. The methods of doing so are very similar to the methods of stopping a catch (pages 92 and 93), but in general if an attacker has created enough space in which to make an immediate shot then the defender should offer a token resistance in order to add to the great difficulties inherent in the shot. These difficulties will do the defender's job for him, and the percentage of such shots scored will be low. Any great attempt by the defender to recover lost ground will result almost inevitably in committing himself into an even worse defensive position—and many times into a foul on the shooter.

2. The Drive

If the attacker believes that he has 'right of way' into a particular space from which he can shoot (a penetration shot), then he will drive strongly and maybe quickly, using a protective dribble (page 61). If, as a complete player, he is to be capable of driving to either side of his opponent, then he MUST be capable of dribbling well with either hand. As he moves into the space he will often ensure maximum ball protection by turning his trunk so that his back is towards the defender, and the leading shoulder down. This position also makes him somewhat slimmer (if he is of normal build), so that he can more easily penetrate a small space. In medium and long range drives, the movement will most often

Plate 65 Thomas beginning a drive; at least one of the defensive methods being used is illegal!

Plate 66 Defender fading backwards and sideways against Dave Hemsley's drive.

start from a front facing working position, and the first bounce of the dribble is the most vulnerable. If the foot furthest from the dribbling hand is used for the first step then it does help the driver to achieve early protection of the ball.

The defender has to decide very quickly whether he should attack the vulnerable early part of the drive, by stepping in and sweeping from low upwards with the furthest arm from the dribbler, or should fade gradually backwards, moving so as to block the further extension of the driving space (Fig. 38).

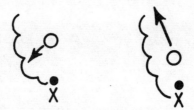

Figure 38

The first of these demands extremely quick movement from the defender, and is dangerous from the foul point of view as any contact will inevitably go against him since he is moving into the attacker. The second manoeuvre is certainly the easiest to perform, and especially if the defender moves quickly he can force the attacker to avoid him by 'steering a more lateral course'. This is called defensive steering, or 'Shutting the Gate', and is the basis of good individual defence. It has the danger that if the defender is greatly committed to his movement, a sudden stop by the attacker will leave the defender floundering on—giving the driver room to perform a height shot (generally a jump shot) instead.

If the defender has managed to 'shut the gate', he will often have committed himself to a movement lateral to the drive in order to do so. At that stage, the attacker can reverse his body position, rolling around to the other side of the defender whilst changing his dribbling hand. The ball is always protected by the body, using a long stride with the back to the defender (Fig. 39).

Figure 39

When well executed, the Offensive Roll is very difficult to stop, since the defender has to suddenly switch to shutting the gate on the other side. He can turn *facing* the driver, but considering his likely stance this is an awkward movement (page 71). It is often better for him to choose the lesser evil of turning away from his man in a Defensive Roll, coming back in fast and low a little later but more safely (Fig. 40).

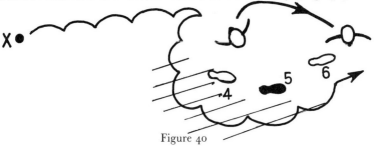

Figure 40

However, when his back is turned the driver has the chance of a quick height shot taken from the area shaded in Fig. 40. One of the major difficulties of the offensive roll is of remaining within the law! The attacker might discover that the defender has moved very quickly and adopted a legal stance

which blocks his (new) intended direction. Since the attacker
has his back to the defender at this time the discovery may
come through a collision—which almost inevitable should be
penalised against the attacker. He also runs the risk of committing an illegal dribble if he carries the ball too far laterally in
changing direction—as most players tend to do. Yes, altogether
a very difficult manoeuvre to perform and oppose—but a
beautiful one when done well.

These basic methods are used in 1 v. 1 play in any court
position, and apply even in the case of centres playing close to
basket. On many occasions, an attacking centre will stand
facing outwards from the basket, so his movements have to be
adapted to this 'reverse' position. He has the commonly added
dimension of moving away from the basket into a shot, either
by stepping away into a hook shot or jumping into a 'Fadeaway' height shot (Fig. 41).

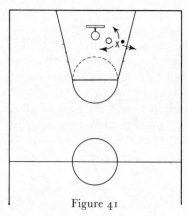

Figure 41

A centre's offensive roll is done really from a fake step
backwards to one side, and then a short drive (including a one
or two bounce dribble) to the other.

Take Off

The driving player is attempting a height or penetration shot,
either of which will almost invariably require him to eventually leave the floor on a lateral or vertical jump. As usual,
the defender is trying to forestall these moves. If a jump

108

shot is performed as a sudden action when the defender is committed to a movement away from the shooter, most of the principles mentioned in the section on immediate shooting apply (page 103). Since the driver already has movement (in a lateral direction), he converts this into vertical movement by bouncing from one or (more usually) two feet, very quickly and with less knee bend than usual. This is called a Stop Jump Shot.

Many players prefer their drive height shot to be a hook shot, especially against a very good defender who has closed the path to basket and is too fast to allow a stop jump shot. The shot is very difficult to check, and there is less need for an element of surprise in the take off. A two count rhythm is generally used, with the foot opposite the shooting hand used as take off foot. (A 'count' occurs as one or both feet simultaneously hit the floor.) If the shooter is moving very fast, the board is often used as a means of softening the ball's flight towards basket (page 42).

Penetration take offs can be divided into two categories— one count or two count. The one count shot uses time as the main method of penetration. By going up on a lateral jump from the *first* step after picking up the ball, the shooter can be first into the air and remain ahead of the defender in the move towards basket. The defender is especially 'caught napping' because he will usually anticipate a two count take off at the end of a drive. Players who have devoted most or all of their practice to two count take offs find it very difficult to acquire the one count skill and there is a great deal to be said for teaching these shots from both one and two counts right from the start.

A two count penetration shot is used in cases where a strong check is anticipated at a certain point on the way in towards basket. This is especially the case when driving past a relatively stationary player, but also is needed when a defender's choice of checking position is predictable. The driver should pick up the ball, either from a dribble or pass, just before reaching the check and take his first count at that point. He must protect the ball strongly, and allow his momentum to carry him through the check. After clearing the check, by which time he has little momentum to enable him to give

Plate 67 Malcolm Campbell on the first pace of his drive take off, using his body for protecting the ball.

power for his throw, he uses the second pace to develop the final drive towards basket.

This technique of a two stage power development for penetration of a strong check is also employed by centres playing under basket. Holding the ball protectively, a centre is usually surrounded by a forest of arms and bodies, through which he has to burst with a very powerful jump. After clearing the clutching defence, he should still have sufficient arm bend from his protective holding position to be able to extend vigorously and propel the ball towards basket (see Plate 21).

In all this we have tended rather to ignore the defender, but he is not helpless in these situations. Whatever his earlier actions have been in coping with an attacking player, as the take off is approached he should attempt to *match* the movements of the shooter. This is easy if the attacker is making a rhythmical and predictable development of the shot, but difficult if the shooter is unpredictable. By moving alongside and in step with the shooter, the defender can often 'feel' the movement which is to occur and either anticipate it slightly or synchronise with it. If the ball is not in a protected position,

Plate 68 Hextall and Hildyard of England match the movements of an opposing Spaniard to check his shot.

then the general rule is 'the earlier the better'. He runs less risk of fouling by using the arm furthest from the shooter in such checks (Fig. 42).

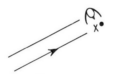

Figure 42

If the ball is protected, then the defender must maintain his similarity of movement with the shooter until the ball eventually does emerge into a vulnerable position. With hook shots the ball might never be vulnerable of course. As soon as the defender can get a hand to the ball he should firstly try just to deflect it enough to cause the shot to miss. This takes only a very slight movement of arm or hand, and is least likely to cause a foul. If, however, the defender is considerably higher than the shooter, he may have the opportunity of a more vigorous movement which can secure possession of the ball by hitting it to a team mate, or even catching it himself.

Most often, in good standard basketball, it is not possible to check shots without fouling. Body movements are so fast, and players so close together, that even the slightest miscalculation can result in contact. Not all the fouls are penalised or even seen—and quite a few are penalised without having even occurred! The fact still remains that fouls on the shooter

Plate 69 Bob McKay is relatively high enough to check the shot after it leaves Carl Olson's hands.

constitute one of the major obstacles to winning games, and it has paid me to teach my players *not to actually check shots*. Occasionally, when one of my boys is considerably taller than his opponent, I am happy to see a well executed check maybe *after* the ball leaves the shooter's hand; but on the whole, checking shots is 'out'.

This does not mean that shooters are allowed free shots *ad nauseam*. The most difficult part of any shot, in terms of achieving accuracy, is the final release of the ball. The defender can afford to ignore that aspect and concentrate on making all the other parts of the shot more difficult. For instance, by good defensive steering the shooter can be made to fade away; by reaching high on the defensive jump the shooter can be forced to over reach himself both vertically and laterally in releasing the ball; by use of moving body and arms the defender can deny the shooter a clear and uninterrupted view of the basket, etc., etc. The total effect of such defence is to greatly increase the difficulty of shots, whilst minimising the risk of committing fouls on the shooter. If a defence can reduce its opponents' shooting percentage from 50 to 45 per cent, a defeat of 100–95 can be turned into a 90–95 victory! This is, of course, a simplified example, but the gains are even greater in terms of:

1. Denying opponents a great number of foul shots (with their specifically higher percentage).
2. Having fewer key players fouled out of the game.

The Pass

Having dealt with the problem of receiving a pass, we must now examine the underlying principles in making one. The passer must first be aware that his team mate wants the ball—either by receiving a signal, or by a prearranged play. He then has to decide which passing lanes are open to him, these depending upon the working position he has adopted with the ball, the defensive stance of his opponent, the position in which his team mate wants the ball, and the deployment of other defenders. When his mind is made up the ball is thrown in one of the ways discussed in pages 35 to 39.

The choice of working position is influenced by many factors, the most important really being the offensive function of the ball handler. If he is *mainly* a passer, then he will hold the ball at a level from which the majority of his passes will be made. With tall team mates this could mean a high level hold, and high plane passes—with tall opponents, vice versa. If he is also a driving player, then his working position will generally be in the middle range, so that he can more quickly begin a dribble and yet still be in a good passing position.

The defender is, of course, attempting to reduce the offensive options (page 101), including the more dangerous passes. However, his defensive stance cannot cut off all eventualities, and there will be gaps through which a ball can be passed. A defender who has his arms well bent is able to move very quickly to block any gaps close to the trunk and head (page 77), so passes are best put wide through gaps. A defender with straight arms cannot move so quickly, and the ball can be thrown much closer to his body through a gap. Balls which are lobbed high, and to a lesser extent which are bounced, are slower passes and much more liable to interception. Their use tends to be restricted to specific situations.

When practising passing, players should look for these gaps (above and to the sides of the head, under the armpits, through and around the legs), and learn to create them by

Plate 70 A typical passing situation. The author has several gaps through which to pass:

a. head height to Pearce (10), beginning to signal for the ball;
b. bounce pass, again to Pearce;
c. hand off to Shaw (6), either automatic or from a call;
d. bounce or high to Williams (11).

fakes of all description. Defenders should continually change their stance, particularly the arm position, so that the passer is faced with an even more difficult situation, but being wary of opening a very dangerous gap in their defence—such as a pass into the centre. However, the defender has just as much right to fake as the attacker, and a fake movement to open a passing lane can very often attract a pass which can be anticipated and intercepted.

One type of pass which has been much neglected in this country is the one made from a baulked shot. Mostly these occur when a shooter has jumped only to discover (what he may have in fact intended) that the defence to his shot is extremely good. The fact that the defence has committed itself, with one or more players, will often mean that a gap exists into which another attacker can move. The problem is then to give the second attacker the ball, and herein lies one of the main reasons for maintaining a two handed grip on the ball for as long as possible during shots. It is easier, with two

114

hands, to move the ball suddenly in a new direction. The passer must also, of course, know just where his team mate is—and this information can be gained from a signal, or by a prearranged tactic.

Blocking Out

Good basketball is a game of controlled possession. The players' ability to control and protect the ball ensures that the majority of possessions result in shots. If we assume that in two fairly even teams the shooting percentages will be similar, then the team taking the greatest number of shots will win. Provided that the teams are also more or less matched in their ability to avoid losing possession without shooting, then the way to get more shots is by getting more possessions. This is done by winning the tussles for the 'uncommitted' ball—that is, when the ball is in the air on a rebound from a missed shot (or, less frequently, on a jump ball).

I have made this little preamble to emphasise the vital importance of one of the most neglected skills in basketball. The early comments on the ball protection (page 22) have shown how one player can be prevented from reaching the ball by the body position of another. This principle can be extended to the rebound situation, where by skilful body positioning a player can deny his opponent access to the ball.

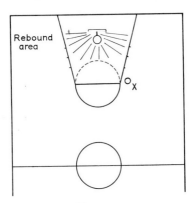

Figure 43

Theoretically, if all five players in a team can do this successfully, then they MUST get the ball!

Taking the blocking out situation on an individual basis, in most cases the defender is most favourably placed to obstruct his opponent—ie. between him and the likely rebound area (Fig. 43). We have seen previously (page 93) that a defender should position himself so that he can see both his man and the ball. However, as soon as the ball has been thrown towards the basket, the defender has less need to be able to see it since *he knows where it is going*. He may then turn his attention more fully towards his opponent, to make up his mind what route the attacker is going to take towards the rebound area.

With one important exception, the situation is now one of defensive steering (page 106). By continually shutting the gate,

Plate 71 At a shot the defender's first duty is to discover where his opponent is going. 4 v 4 illustrates this point.

Plate 72 Defender has ignored Terry Keogh's hook shot, and has turned to block out.

116

Plate 73 Pete Tidey blocks out Carl Olson to take the ball.

the defender prevents the attacker from achieving a particularly advantageous floor position. But, since the ultimate aim of the defender is to catch the ball, it is necessary at some stage to turn and face the rebound area, maybe even losing sight of the attacker altogether. The technique used is the defensive roll (page 107), performed when the defender estimates the ball is just rebounding and when he knows which side the attacker is trying to get by. By rolling *away* from the attacker, but *into* his intended path, the defender can ensure that any ensuing foul is committed by the attacker (who in his eagerness may push the defender in the back)—or at least that he can feel where the attacker is (on his back!) even though he cannot see him.

If the roll is well timed, the defender can come immediately from his crouched position into a jump for the ball, being perfectly placed to reach for it without having to worry about fouling his man. It may be, of course, that the ball will not rebound in his direction, but if his four team mates are well positioned and have each blocked their man out, then one of them will be in a good position to snare the ball.

The blocking out situation is somewhat complicated for centres playing close to basket. Certainly from positions on the edge of the key the same moves apply, but if the play is just under the basket, 'in line' defence is not used, so blocking out becomes virtually impossible. In this case, the centre relies on his timing and jumping ability to get the ball, being merely wary that he is not forced into a position *under* the ring otherwise the ball will always rebound away from him.

In all this action, the attacker is not entirely left without possibilities. If he is facing a good 'blocker out', then he can use two basic plays. Firstly, he can delay his cut, faking the defender into a defensive roll and then swerving to the blind side. Secondly, he can by repeated advancing fakes, cause the defender to retreat so far into the rebound area that the ball will tend to rebound out over his head. The attacker has the great advantage of being able to see clearly where he is going, and also to have the ball within his field of vision. He tries to force the defender to commit himself—and as usual, the best man will win, helped by good techniques and a little bit of luck!

The Individual Contribution

The great majority of foregoing comment has been concerned with the individual, performing basketball skills usually in close harness with an opponent. The individual's total contribution to the game depends mainly upon his ability to perform these skills well. Many of the things he has to do will be almost automatic reactions to situations, to which the knowledgeable coach will expose him many times during training. This does not mean that the player is an automaton in what he does, because automatons are predictable in their responses—and the predictable player is easier to oppose. No, the automatic aspect of a player's reactions to play situations should always be governed by an intelligent ability to vary things (slightly or greatly). But a player cannot be expected to think about *everything* which is happening. He must be able to leave the automatic things to themselves, putting his concentration on the 'key' aspects of a situation, maybe changing course at the last moment—but in full knowledge that his 'automatic' reactions will adapt to the new instructions he is giving.

Herein lies the difference between the competent but stereotyped individual, and the thinking genius of the ball court.

Combined Play

At this stage, we are not yet thinking of total team play, but of two or more team mates combining in play. The importance here is to realise that combined play is only useful if it achieves benefits which the individuals acting alone would be unable to achieve. It seems foolish to make players undertake the vastly more complex and difficult adjustments to combined play unless there is a necessity and an ability for it.

Basketball has a long history of pendulum swinging between simple individual and complex group play. I have no special brief for either, but I do suffer the tortures of the damned when I see coaches destroying the effectiveness of their team play because of a blind insistence that the means are more important than the ends. How many times do we see players stifling their natural abilities, turning down great scoring chances while struggling in a morass of predetermined moves? Meanwhile the coach bubbles on the bench, screaming 'Ya gotta play the play', and withdrawing any player to the bench who has had the temerity to ignore instructions and score by a 'non approved' method! I have seen it many times, with regret. I have also seen—many times—players trying to win games on their own, and failing, when a trust and co-operation with their team mates would have achieved far more. I have not only seen it, I have *done* it, and *still* do it when a clutch situation causes me to lose some self control. It is easy for authors to pontificate, harder for participants to achieve the proposed perfections in play!

The reason we play as teams, even in sports having two man teams (tennis, tag wrestling, etc.), is that the whole should be greater than the sum of the parts. If five players, each having

'100 units' of effectiveness, get together on court, the total effect should be 600 units, or 700 . . . or more. And yet it is possible for the total effect to be 400, 300, 0 . . . or even minus!

The coaches task is to maximise this effect, by a combination of physical, physiological and psychological means. My job in this book is to examine mainly the physical means.

Since we are involved in a metaphysical train of thought, it might be a good idea to consider in a little more detail some of the underlying concepts to this 'combined play'.

Commitment

We have continually found ourselves up against this aspect of individual play, and it forms a central theme of group plays as well. If the opposition can be forced to commit itself to one course of action, it cannot change that course even though it later becomes obvious that it will fail. It *will* fail, only if counter moves of sufficient power are taken, without the opposition realising that they have been, or will be taken. If the counter moves are not powerful enough, then the 'committed' action may be successful, and the opposition's commitment will have paid off—for them. So, one analyses a situation, decides that a particular counter move would be very powerful, *and encourages the opposition to commit itself to the manoeuvre which will be negated by the counter move.* For instance, an extremely high jumper might deliberately leave an opponent open for a jump shot, jumping as soon as the shooter is committed to leaving the floor, and catching the ball or slapping it away *after* it has left the shooter's hand.

Prediction

The few comments on page 110 indicated that players should try not to be predictable in their actions. If one can predict what the opposition will do, one can take early steps to counteract this play. The balance of effectiveness between opponents will then depend upon two things:

    1.   The ability to recognise cues in opponents' play showing that certain actions will take place.

2. The ability to disguise one's own actions, hiding cues from the opponents, or giving false cues as fakes.

Most players achieve a certain degree of prediction ability purely through experience—however, a coach should teach both his players and himself to be more discriminating in the search for and observation of cues.

Probability

Basketball is a game of success and failure. Players try to improve the balance between the two, and essentially are concerned with *increasing* the probability of success in all the actions they take. Also, they must be concerned with *decreasing* the probability of success in their opponents' actions. In the modern game of basketball it is realised that it is impossible to prevent opponents from shooting. In this case, defence ought to restrict opponents to where shooting percentage is low. This will not ensure that no score will ensue but that relatively few shots will score. On the other hand, if a shooter can encourage a defender to make an aggressive attempt to check a shot, then the probability of a foul being committed will be high. So, the attacker shoots in such a way as to maximise the joint probabilities of scoring and being fouled. Not only does he stand a chance of scoring, and of getting two foul shots if he misses (and a bonus foul shot even if he does score, under American rules), but also of getting his opponent fouled out of the game sooner.

So, we can now see that basketball consists of predicting one's opponent's actions sufficiently to encourage him to commit himself to a probability of failure! In this frame of mind I should like to explore the various permutations of group play, until arriving at the final analysis of team play.

Balanced Play

This category of play deals with situations where individual superiority is not sufficient to ensure a high probability of success. The opposing forces are to a certain extent balanced, individual for individual, group for group.

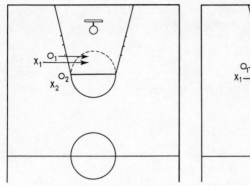
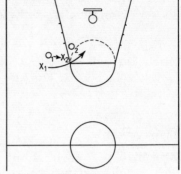

Figure 44   Figure 45

2 v 2. Consider first the offensive aim—to get one of the players into a position, with the ball, from where he can take a high percentage shot. The defence wants to prevent this (Fig. 44). If X_1 attempts to cut into the key, O_1 will shut the gate and steer X_1 away from the danger area. X_2 has a legal method of preventing O_1 from moving in any given direction, that is by positioning himself on the intended route, making himself a Screen (Fig. 45). O_1, if he attempts to follow X_1 closely, must collide with either X_2 or O_2; *provided* that X_1 runs very close to X_2, X_1 then loses his defender. The screen can be made more certain if X_1 fakes in the wrong direction before running off the screen (Fig. 46).

Figure 46

The problem of having X_1 with the ball can be solved in one of three ways:

1. By X_1 having the ball to start with, in which case he must dribble it (protectively) during the manoeuvre.
2. By X_2 having the ball, and giving a hand off pass to X_1 as he moves around the screen.
3. By X_1 receiving a pass from some other team mate at any stage during the acceptance of the screen.

Good shooting positions are shown shaded in the figures accompanying these descriptions. The screen is essentially a convergent play (page 87) which uses the convergence of team mates and of opponents to provide obstacles for the

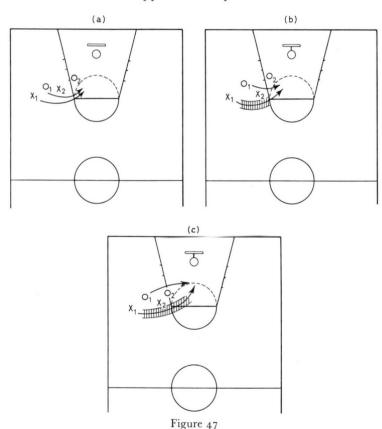

Figure 47

defence. At the time these obstacles become effective, the screening player can be moving or stationary. If moving, it must be *legal* movement!

Defenders must be aware of the dangers of convergent situations, and adapt their normal movements in order to minimise the effectiveness of obstructions. They must gather as much information about the situation as possible by peripheral vision, warnings from team mates, feeling behind them for obstructions (illegal in some basketball circles), and prediction of likely offensive moves. Three counters to an attempted screen are shown in Figure 47.

a. Going 'Over The Top' of the screen. The defender, if quick enough, can get there first—forcing the attacker to run wide of the screen. Dangerous if the attacker goes the other way (left) when the defender has committed himself.

b. 'Sliding' through between the screen and the defender's team mate, who steps back to allow the slider room to pass. Dangerous against a stop jump shot over the screen.

c. 'Sagging' behind the screen and team mate. Economical in terms of effort, but very dangerous in that it increases the opportunities for the shooter.

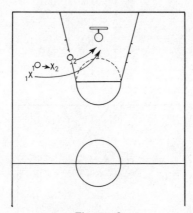

Figure 48

If the defender attempts to go over the top, or merely collides with the screen because he is unable to avoid it, then X_1 is unmarked and a great offensive threat. In that case O_2, who from his advantageous position should have seen all the

Plate 74 Convergence of 20 and 42 creates a screen; 5 cannot follow; 20 is free for an immediate shot; 8 sees the danger and begins an automatic switch.

action, must assume responsibility for the defence of X_2; in fact, he Switches men (Fig. 48 and Plate 74).

He will, hopefully, have been telling O_1 about the screen, and will then tell him that he has switched. If, during the switch O_2 thinks that X_1 may perform a stop jump shot, then he will step around towards the shooter to handicap the take off—but to attempt a check would be very risky in terms of fouling or of committing himself *away* from basket. If O_2 thinks X_1 will drive, then he must *blend* into X_1's pathway, shutting the gate without fouling. Sometimes, O_1 can help O_2 get started by pushing him in the required direction.

A defender who can predict very accurately the outcome of a convergence can in fact anticipate and jump very quickly into the driver's path. This is called a Jump Switch, and can be very disconcerting to the attacker, to say the least!

The discerning reader will by now have noticed from Figure 48 that the screening player, X_2, is nearer to the basket than O_1,

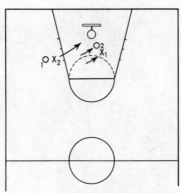

Figure 49

who must assume defensive responsibility for X_2. If the switch has been effective (ie. that X_1 has been countered) then X_2 must press home this positional advantage by cutting towards the basket (Fig. 49). This movement is called a Roll. The trigger which sends him on his way is generally the contact as O_1 collides, or the knowledge that a switch has been effected—which news is given when O_2 calls 'Switch'. As he wants to start quickly, it helps if he is already facing the basket. A screen should therefore be set facing the intended direction of the roll, the total sequence being called a Screen and Roll (or Pick and Roll).

During the roll X_2 needs the ball. Again, he can have it by one of three routes:

1. He may already be holding it, and merely fake to give a hand off as X_1 passes him on the screen.

2. He may give to X_1 on the screen, and receive it back after the switch. This gives more options to score, allowing X_1 the first chance. However, the return pass is often difficult, needing sometimes a height pass (especially from a baulked shot), or more often a bounce pass to either side of O_2 depending upon his position.

3. He may receive a pass from another team mate.

The fourth move in this particular play sequence is a Defensive Roll. As X_2 cuts for basket in Figure 49 O_1 can turn towards the play and follow behind him, defensively a very weak position. On the other hand, since X_2 is either coping

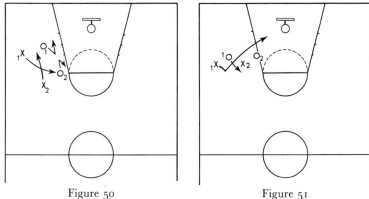

Figure 50   Figure 51

with an awkward dribble, or a difficult pass reception, O_1 can cut his losses by rolling *away* from the play with a long rearward step and coming back in on his opponent as described on page 107.

These four moves (Screen, Switch, Offensive Roll, Defensive Roll) are sufficiently necessary to warrant 'automatic' practice; and yet sufficiently predictable to be upset by unusual variations. The more common of these variations are:

1. Automatic switch *before* the screen is effective (Fig. 50 and Plate 74). The two defenders might merely touch hands as a signal. With good team work this is a very economical move.

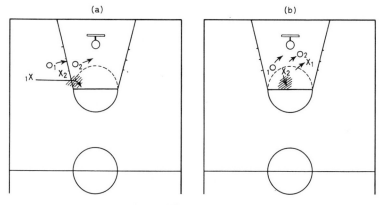

Figure 52

2. Driving the 'wrong side' of the screen (Fig. 51). Good against 'anticipating' defenders. Also a basic error of impatient beginners on offence!

3. The 'step back' (Fig. 52). Used in (a) against a retreating defence to a screen, and (b) against an anticipatory switch and defensive roll. Both step back situations give an opportunity for an immediate shot.

One could continue *ad infinitum* (or *ad nauseam*) with these combinations of moves, but the ones mentioned are the more common *planned* plays. Any players performing these really well are ready for international basketball!

Many teams never get beyond 2 man plays, in fact, even the best teams in the world operate mainly on such combined manoeuvres from various pairs at given times. Bringing in a third player greatly increases the complexity of the situation. For example, let us take a hypothetical situation (Fig. 53).

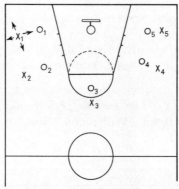

Figure 53

X_1 can go in any one of four directions. In each of these his defender can either follow him or not, so there are $(4 \times 2) = 8$ possibilities in the X_1–O_1 situation.

If we include X_2 in the set up, for each of those possibilities X_2 can also move in one of four directions—followed or not followed by O_2. Therefore the possible eventualities are $8 \times (4 \times 2) = 64$. If X_3 and O_3 come into the play, the total becomes $64 \times (4 \times 2) = 512$. Now, the players know that many of these eventualities occur so rarely that they can be discounted, but if we accept the figures as indicative of the relative difficulty in analysing the situation, then we shan't be far wrong.

Now, as X_1 and X_2 go through their offensive manoeuvre, which might only take a couple of seconds, the possibilities are gradually being eliminated as the players spot the important cues. Eventually, there might only be two or three possible actions from which the players have to choose. The chances of success are high, even though initially there were 64 possibilities. Bringing in an extra player (from one to two) had only increased the options by $64 - 8 = 56$.

However, bring in a third player and the extra options total $512 - 64 = 448$. Altogether a different picture, at which the mind boggles!

Of course, this dreadfully oversimplified picture isn't much like the real game, but the concept underlying it is a valid one. Coaches have to devise ways of limiting the options so that their players are not bemused by the sheer weight of information surrounding them. In our case, if three men have to be brought into a play situation, by giving the third man instructions such as 'Pass' or 'Don't Pass' his situation is reduced to two options, *only* doubling the total options in the play. We have already mentioned that on the two man plays where neither attacker had the ball, the final pass was made by 'another player' (page 126). This is the third man, imposing an extra load which is just bearable, provided his contribution to the play is a worthwhile one. One can call this a transitional play, more than two man but not fully three man (Fig. 54).

Figure 54

The reader will recognise all the movements on the left hand side as those of the Screen and Roll of Figure 49. To them, we have merely added a pass to and from the third man, the whole play now becoming a 'Screen Off the Ball', or Screen and Roll Off the Ball. The first pass (move 1) can be the signal to start, and then the second pass (move 4) becomes critical in its timing. If not correctly made, the play breaks down. This is not a catastrophe, since in a well trained team this very move might occur over 200 times in one game, and they are not all going to result in a basket being scored. We must allow the defence to triumph occasionally—just to add spice to the game!

Post Play

An adaptation of the last play (where two players move and the third remains stationary to pass the ball), is that developed around a stationary player at a medium distance from basket (Fig. 55). Here X_3 is the post player, usually a centre, but sometimes another player who has been forced to stop during a move towards basket. The post has the ball, either by dribbling it in, or by having it passed to him, and faces away from his pressing defender in a protective stance. X_1 and X_2 cut in a curving path, diagonally in front of the post, one immediately after the other. When performed well, considerable defensive confusion can be caused by the proliferation of obstacles, and there is a probability that one

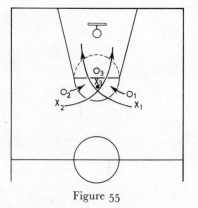 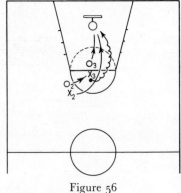

Figure 55   Figure 56

or more of the three attackers will get free. If this is X_1 or X_2 then X_3 either gives him a hand off pass while he passes in front of the screen(s), or a bounce or height pass after he has cleared the melee. If X_3 is free, he can either take an immediate shot, or drive around *behind* one of his team mates (Fig. 56). As usual, in screen plays, this is an extremely convergent situation. Not only is a screen provided by the stationary X_3, but X_1 and X_2 screen for one another when they cross *and* they both can screen for X_3 if he drives. These latter are all moving screens, and great care must be taken to ensure that the movements are made in a legal manner—dependent upon local interpretations of the fouling rules.

Though post plays offer most advantages when situated at the top of the key, they can be performed in any position, and with one, two, three or even four cutting players.

Weave Play

A third adaptation of group convergence is seen in weave play. The strict weave (Fig. 57) is seen *par excellence* in the performances of demonstration teams, especially our old friends the Harlem Globetrotters. In (a) the stationary weave, the ball is protected from defenders (real or imaginary) by being held, dribbled or passed on the side away from basket. The passes are all made within the 'D', from the player leaving to the player entering the 'D'. In the full court weave (b) the ball advances down court, always being passed forward to the player cutting in from the side. It is mainly used for practice, and assumes that the defenders are not close. Such perfect, and continuous, weave plays are rarely seen during games, but the weave concept of convergence can be demonstrated by two or more players in cuts towards basket and circulation afterwards (Fig. 58). This type of movement has a certain (and rather *ad hoc*) attraction about it, providing a smooth and flowing shift of play without too much formalism, and allowing scope for each player to express his own individual personality and talents. It provides innumerable opportunities for screen plays, but it is necessary that the ball should also flow around the players, without necessarily having to move too much around the court. In this case, the ball's position can

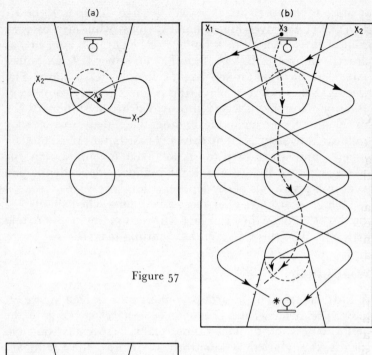

Figure 57

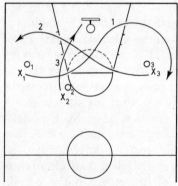

Figure 58

be very near the ultimately desired high percentage shooting area—more or less hovering there, waiting for the chance to pounce.

The strict weave is too predictable to be successful in a game; a defender can merely step in and gum up the works! The less formal weaves work even though they are three man plays, largely because if you keep running in that fashion for long enough (generally a few seconds) chance will get someone free. But, the players have to be very able in their performance of individual fundamentals to maintain such movement patterns and yet keep their attention primed for the chance when it comes.

Overload

'Get there first with the most' is a good maxim in war and games. What exactly is meant by 'the most' depends upon the relative superiority of numbers, armament, skill, etc. A general arriving at the battlefield with 10,001 soldiers against 10,000 opponents might be forgiven for not feeling entirely confident in the overwhelming superiority of his numbers—especially if his men only had clubs to oppose the automatic rifles of their foes!

Many basketball coaches would consider one good player versus one inferior player an 'overload', but since we are at the moment concerned with group play, we shall look at the numerical overload situations where players are of equal ability, but continually being aware that in actual play the situation will be modified by the relative abilities of the players.

1 v 0. We discussed the implication of the free shot situation on page 50, and quite obviously the easiest way to score is to get one man away on his own, ending up with a free shot from under the basket. Since most of our overload offence is designed to give one player a free shot, though not necessarily from under the basket, we must be aware that the 1 v 0 situation should be contrived in an area where there is a *high probability of scoring*. In all overload offences, the aim should be to get the defence to commit itself in such a way that a high scoring area is left open, into which a free attacker can move. Naturally, the defence will be unwilling to play along with this, and a *great reluctance to commitment* is the essence of defence against overload.

2 v 1. The most effective tactic against an overladen defence is divergence (page 87). Whilst convergence *can* be used, it certainly makes defence easier for the skilful player. Since a defender is unwilling to commit himself in low scoring areas,

he will essentially have a tendency to move back towards the basket, making screen play a poor proposition. On the other hand, a divergent offensive approach imposes upon a defender the necessity of having to move fast in order to be able to cover whichever of two or more opponents has the ball. However, the defender's duty to press the ball handler is inversely proportional to the ball's distance from the basket, since he is unwilling to commit himself in low scoring areas. Figure 59

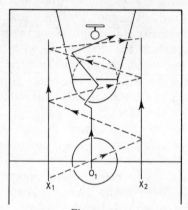

Figure 59

shows two attackers advancing against a defender, passing the ball between one another. In a non-shooting area, the defender should ignore them and concentrate on retreating quickly. As the attackers near the high percentage shooting areas, the defender must move ever more firmly in the direction of the ball handler, but never committing himself to anything other than the defence of a lay up shot.

The difficulty of the defender's task can really be appreciated by measuring the ground covered in a situation such as Figure 59. Here the defender has covered about 25 per cent more ground than the attackers, in addition to the problems of having to run backwards. The offence *should* be able to either overtake the defender, or to be able to time a pass precisely enough to catch the defender moving in the wrong direction. The pass receiver should then be cutting into the basket, giving the defender an impossible task of turning and moving across in sufficient time to check the shot. Figure 60 shows the

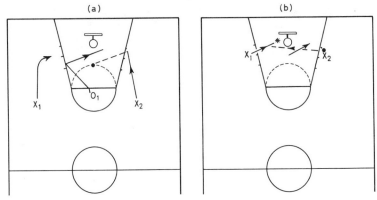

(a)   (b)

Figure 60

final stages of the movement illustrated in Figure 59, but with the offence making the telling move. (a) shows X_1 and O_1 moving in the same direction and at the same time as the ball, towards X_2. He then returns the ball immediately to X_1 who takes it in his stride for a lay up, whereas O_1 has been forced to commit himself away from X_1 and cannot switch positions in time.

As seen on page 80, passing the ball slows the two offensive players' movement down court. It is useful only if a poor defender is reacting to the ball's movement in mid court. On the other hand, if one attacker is appreciably in front of the other, he must be given the ball if possible (Fig. 61). He will then drive for basket, only passing to his team mate if he is prevented

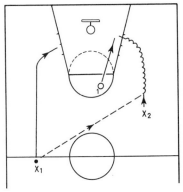

Figure 61

Plate 75 Beginning of a 3 v 1 overload. The defender has made the mistake of challenging mid court.

from reaching a good shooting position, he should *not* stop dribbling otherwise the defender will be free to switch. The final angle at which X_1 should approach the basket will depend upon the finishing position of X_2 and O_1 and will generally be towards the free side of the shooting area.

3 v 1. A sensible defender will retreat under his own basket, and commit himself only to the defence of a lay up. In this case the offence merely want to get the ball up court as quickly as possible, which is best done by the centre player dribbling. He has then the option of selecting the side to which the ball shall be passed (Fig. 62). Having this option allows him to fake in an effort to move the defender to the wrong side, and to select the most likely scorer. In some cases he can fake the defender so well that he is free to lay the ball in himself! Once having

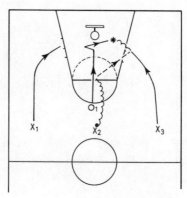

Figure 62

passed, X_2 should remain just outside the defended area. The recipient of the pass tries, of course, to drive—but if stopped by a committed defender he can then pass to a cutting X_1 or a more or less stationary X_2. If X_2 is within the key, he must either shoot immediately, or get out, to avoid a 3 second violation.

Plate 76 2 v 1 overload, with the retreating defender faking to slow down the dribbler until defensive help arrives.

In each of these single defender cases (2 v 1 and 3 v 1), the defender can also fake by making fierce movements towards the ball handler and then immediately retreating to the likely pass recipient. The ball handler can often be encouraged to stop dribbling in this way, giving the defender better odds against the rest of the offence (1 v 1 or 1 v 2). However, if the defender does commit himself more to the others, he must adopt a stance which will prevent the ball being passed (page 92). Otherwise, the ball handler may immediately pass and cut into a free position for a return pass.

137

E*

3 v 2. As one would expect, the addition of yet another player to the overload situation increases the complexity greatly. I should like, therefore, to categorize the play options into:

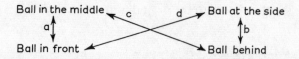

These possibilities are illustrated in Figure 63.

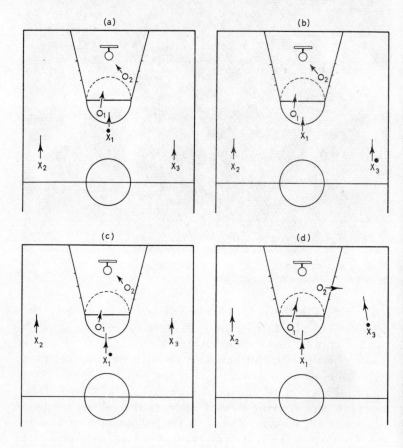

Figure 63

Of course, the ball can be passed between attackers, which immediately changes the type of formation, but these categories describe the formation at the time the defence is being encouraged to commit itself. Since the odds are slightly better, as far as the defence is concerned, it is more willing to commit one man to the ball handler at a greater distance from the basket. This distance will depend upon many factors, one of the most important being the attacker's shooting accuracy from that distance. In general, attackers should expect to be challenged quite strongly up to 15 feet from the basket.

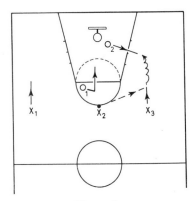

Figure 64

Two defenders will normally play 'Tandem' defence, where O_1 will challenge the ball handler, and try to make him stop dribbling at a long distance from the basket (Fig. 64). Having achieved that, O_1 retreats to a mid key position. X_2 will pass to one side, the receiver being challenged by O_2. If he is stopped then O_1 will challenge the next attacker to receive a pass, whilst O_2 retreats to mid key. By then, help should have arrived to overcome the overload situation. This essentially delaying tactic can be most effective if the defenders achieve a co-ordinated alternation of one going out to the ball while the other falls back.

When it becomes obvious to the defenders that one or other category (Fig. 63) offence is being used, they should adapt their position to put O_1 nearest the ball handler. So, a 'ball at the side' offence would find the defenders deployed across the

139

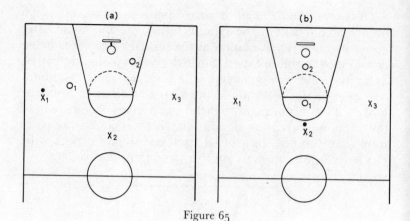

Figure 65

court; a 'ball in the middle' offence should result in a 'fore and aft' defence (Fig. 65).

The offence against tandem defence should not assume that it will get a close free shot, though it might occasionally happen if the defence makes a bad error. Rather should it aim at producing a fairly close free shot, or a drive from a very favourable position. It acknowledges that whereas 1 v 0 is 95 per cent probable and 2 v 1 90 per cent probable of scoring, 3 v 2 cannot hope for much more than 75 per cent probability (these figures being imaginary examples to illustrate the point).

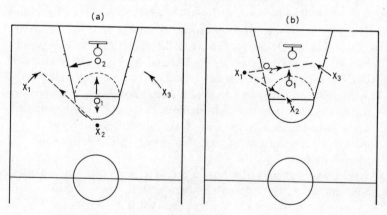

Figure 66

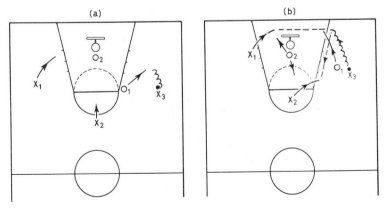

Plate 77 3 v 2 ball ahead at side overload. Defenders have erred in both covering 7 who, having committed the defence, passes off to 11. This plate is interesting in that it was coincidentally taken a fraction of a second after Plate 16, which reinforces this analysis!

Because it is unlikely that the rear line of the tandem will fail to defend the basket, the essential aspect of the offence is to commit the outside defender into a bad position. Figure 66 (a) shows the centre ball handler stopped by O_1, the pass out to X_1 with the shuttle by O_2 to cover him. As the ball is on its way, O_1 shuttles to become the new rear line of defence. Figure 66 (b) shows the next development, where O_2 is committed outside, and O_1 committed to the basket. X_1 has two

Figure 67

141

choices to pass. A difficult pass to X_3 gives him a reasonable opportunity to drive. An easier pass to X_2 creates a good chance for an immediate shot (with X_3 already on the move for a rebound if the shot misses).

Figure 67 shows a ball on the side situation, where the ball handler drives as far as he can towards the baseline and into basket. He will almost inevitably be stopped, but will have firmly committed O_1 to a position away from basket and yet near enough to leave O_2 in serious doubt about his function. Having stopped X_3, O_1 cannot retreat since X_3 would shoot. O_2 might decide to go towards either X_1 or X_2, leaving the other free for a pass and an immediate shot.

Higher Orders

Where the 'firstest with mostest' principles are extended to 4 v 2, 4 v 3, 5 v 3 and 5 v 4, the situation becomes understandably complex. At this stage it would be better for us to consider that the offence is unlikely to come as four or five men abreast. Generally two or three will have made a first move followed by others of the team. This is called a Two (or more) Wave Offence.

The first wave in such offence is often countered by the defence, in which case one of the attackers will be holding the ball *or will have taken an unsuccessful shot*. The second wave of offence should then come through very powerfully, having selected the best routes through the somewhat disorientated defence. They are expecting to penetrate the defence, and only have the problem of getting the ball. Figure 68 (a) shows the situation where the first wave has been stopped, and X_4 (backed by X_5) has cut off X_1 who could easily give him a hand off pass. O_1 could not switch quickly enough to stop the fast moving X_4. O_2 would face a 2 v 1 situation then, against X_2 and X_4. Figure 68 (b) illustrates the occasion when the second wave concentrates on 'crashing the boards' for a possible immediate tip in shot, if X_2 happens to miss his shot.

These two situations also illustrate another vital aspect of overload play. If the defence *should* manage to gain possession of the ball from an interception or rebound, then the boot is suddenly on the other foot. A 3 v 2 disadvantage at one end

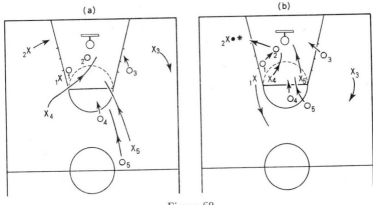

Figure 68

of the court means a 2 v 3 advantage at the other, and a quick retaliation is often a worthwhile tactic to use against a fallible overload offence. For that reason, first wave players who are not directly concerned with the scoring opportunity should come back away from the basket—thus maintaining Defensive Balance. X_1 and X_3 are the players concerned in Figure 68 (b).

TEAM OFFENCE AND DEFENCE

Inevitably we have become involved with more players in our consideration of combined play, until now we are at the stage where we can begin to think of all five players as a team—or rather, all ten players as two teams. I must reiterate as strongly as I can—team play is built from the fundamental play discussed in the earlier parts of this book. Without those fundamental skills, team skill is impossible. Without having ensured that players can perform those skills well, a coach is doomed to frustration if he expects his team to play well. Conversely, a coach should never devise team tactics which demand more skill from his players than they possess. One glorious illustration of this point happened in an international match many years ago. A hastily formed Welsh team were opposing England at a great disadvantage in terms of sophistication and ability, but full of Celtic fervour and ready to die for the cause! Their new coach, George Wilkinson, said to one of the (typically small and wiry) Welsh players 'Now Taffy, I want you to go on and set screens for Vaughan'. The immediate reply—'What's a screen?' 'Well, you run around Vaughan so that he can bump his defender onto you'. This was accepted, and lo and behold on the next offence, there was Taffy running in tight little circles around Vaughan rather like an anxious bee round a flower! Vaughan could hardly move, let alone manufacture screens from the pirouettes of his devoted team mate.

Over the intervening years, players and coaches have developed out of all recognition; and yet there is still a great tendency for coaches to expect too much from players. It is praiseworthy for coaches to set their sights high, but only if the basic ability of the players can match the visions of the coach. If you have 'sow's ear' players, don't expect 'silk purse' play from them. Rather capitalise on the inherent strength of the sow's ear, and abrade the silk of the opposition till it loses its sheen! An average coach can take the best players to victory—a great coach can win with inferior teams.

Basketball is played mainly at the ends of courts. Except for occasional special tactics, the middle of the court is an area which is 'passed through' rather than 'played in'. The nature of the play which takes place at any end must be decided by someone or other, and it is easy to become involved in a 'chicken or egg' conundrum, trying to decide whether the defence or offence has the greatest effect. But when you look at the situation closely, it becomes apparent that the defence are the ones who have to make up their minds what type of game to play. They analyse the abilities and disposition of their opponents, knowing that their job is to *match any patterns* which the offence create. They can settle upon a defensive plan. On the other hand, the offence have the task of creating overload, but the methods they will use cannot be decided until they *know* what form of defence is opposing them. Efficient scouting may have given them a very good idea of what to expect, and plans may be laid in advance, but the first part of play, especially after tactical breaks (ie. beginning of the game, timeouts, half time), must be concerned with checking the form of the defence.

Well prepared teams will of course have their defence

settled before starting to play, and will also have a few optional methods of offence in hand selecting the necessary one *after* evaluating the opposing defence. The number of possibilities is not large. In fact, there are only two *basic* forms of defence, though there are many variation of these forms.

Essentially our discussion of fundamental basketball has centred so far around the interface between two men, a Man-for-Man situation. This concept of play has been developed by the subsequent addition of players, until eventually we can have five defenders—each opposing a particular opponent on a man-for-man basis. The defence may still use support in the case of overladen players, but essentially each player has a prime responsibility to stop one opponent from scoring. Man-for-man defence is a perfectly natural extension of individual fundamentals, is the simplest concept to give beginners, and the easiest defence to play against evenly matched opponents.

Occasionally, team defence will find itself up against an offence with either one or two outstanding superior players, or a team which is generally superior but which lacks talent in one important department. Against such offences, it can often pay off to use a defence which gives players a responsibility for defending a certain floor area. Each defender is given an approximate Zone, in which he knows that he must defend any ball handler. The five zones are so designed as to cover the area in which the offence want to shoot, and theoretically the defence knows that whichever area the ball is in, it will be defended. The point which is all too often forgotten is that within any zone the defence against the ball handler will be completely according to the *fundamental principles of individual defence*.

At this point I should like to digress briefly and discuss the implications of team defence in the development of beginners. Not only is man-for-man defence an easier concept for beginners to understand than zone, but it impresses upon each defender his total individual involvement in his team's efforts and gives him a greater intensity of practice for individual defensive skills. The game is more attractive, can be played 3 v 3, 4 v 4, 5 v 5, 6 v 6 etc. without really altering its nature, and allows each player to feel involved in an individual contest with his opponent as well as in the overall contest between teams. Throughout the world there are many instances of enlightened league organisations who ban zone defence for young players. The ultimate benefits in development of players and teams are plain to see.

As we shall see later, a much higher degree of team collaboration is needed to play zone defence. At the stage when players are sufficiently advanced to be able to manage zone, the exercise of developing complex defensive movements can be most beneficial. Zone defence also confers extra defensive benefits which cannot be achieved so easily with man-for-man, at its best it can give offensive players the feeling that they are playing in a large bowl of syrup!

Man-for-Man Team Defence

We have seen (page 101) that defence decides which are the most dangerous options of the offence, and adopts a stance which decreases the probability of success in these options. Within the total team defence each individual may have different instructions which depend upon the characteristics of his opponent. Let me use an example to illustrate this *extremely important point*.

In 1965, Wales won the 'home countries' international championship, against all the odds. Her rather scanty preparation had been concentrated on achieving flexible defensive systems, leaving offensive to the individual inspiration and ability of the players from a basic team floor position. During the tournament Wales used no less than seven different defences, and yet her opponents, particularly England and Scotland, persisted with stereotyped defences operating on a general principle, without each defender having specific instructions concerning his 'variations on the main theme'. Wales had a young giant in 6 ft 9 in. Smith who should not have been played closely except right under the basket, a fiery little forward in Barclay who should have been encouraged to shoot from outside but prevented at all costs from driving to the right. A converted athlete, 6 ft 5 in. Green, had little sophistication but tremendous physical power, and should have been played closely around the key so that he could be blocked out from rebounds. Quarter back Thomas had a tendency to do everything himself, and should have been pressurised all over the court into weak offensive situations. At 6 ft 5 in. and 210 lb., Williams could do anything if he got the ball near the Key—obviously should have been half or even full fronted as soon as he moved towards the basket.

But—what did Wales find against them? Absolutely standard defences, operating in a kind of half-hearted no-man's-land between fierce pressure and relaxation. Each individual defender found the general defensive instructions given to the team insufficient to cope with the peculiar talents of his particular opponent. And Wales won—easily.

It is obviously necessary to have an overall defensive plan—**but individuals must be given specific instructions within that plan.**

Pressing Man-for-Man

Such defence can be used by a team whose each individual is stronger than his opponent, or as a shock tactic to encourage offences into flustered errors. Each defender stands close to his opponent, to stop him shooting if he has the ball, to prevent him receiving a pass, or to prevent him reaching a good offensive position. Since the distance players are apart is minimised, the distance advantage of the defender (page 96) is lost. He needs to be extremely alert and capable to prevent his opponent cutting past him into a space (X_1 and O_1 in Fig. 69). The dangers can be reduced if the defender half fronts so that the attacker's cut is on the far side away from the ball (X_2 and O_2 in Fig. 69).

A pressing man-for-man is, of course, the perfect way to match an offensive pattern, but extremely susceptible to overload on an individual basis. Just one star attacker can shatter the defense, because there is very little possibility of support. If an attacker can get clear of his defender, he can often go all the way to basket—and this is the first method of offence against a press. Taken to its natural extreme it becomes a Clear Play, where the ball is taken by or given to a star player in a position such as that in Figure 70. He then knows that if he can go round his man, he *must* be clear for a drive shot.

If they have no outstanding overload individual to call upon,

147

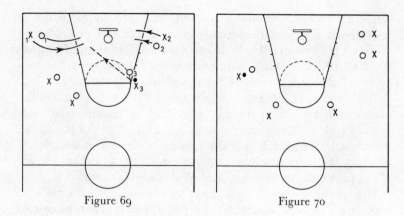

Figure 69　　　　　　　　Figure 70

the offence should then use convergence as the basis of their attack. Screens and pick-and-roll will tend to be most successful, especially if the 'Clear' principle is still used—preventing the shooting area from becoming 'clogged with other "bodies", whether friend or foe!' (Fig. 71).

Alternatively, post plays can be very effective *provided* the ball can be passed safely into the post. The 'clear' can still be maintained by first wave offence coming out wide as the second wave of cutters come in (Fig. 72).

In certain situations, the press can be extended to cover a greater area of court than usual. These presses are described

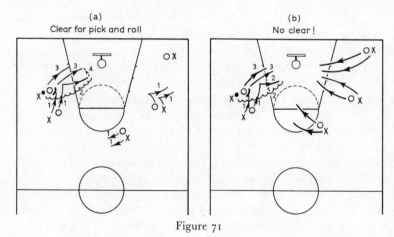

Figure 71

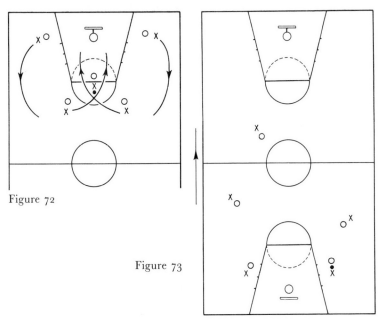

Figure 72

Figure 73

by the court area involved, eg., Full Court Press, Half Court Press, etc. As the press becomes extended beyond the normal shooting area, the defender's stance must be modified since he does not have to stop a shot. A slightly lower carriage can be adopted, which helps the defender to achieve the greater mobility he needs. There will also be a greater tendency to front the attacker, since his chances of going 'Backdoor' are less, ie. for him to cut behind the defender towards the basket. However, the chance is still there, so the defender must be sure to keep his man in vision at all times. Figure 73 shows a typical full court pressing position.

Here, the offence can still apply the standard techniques of Figure 74.

If these manoeuvres are performed carefully, then the press will fail, but if the attackers become flustered, really alert defenders can tie them up into held ball, violations or possession losses. In this case, the jump switch (page 125) becomes a very potent weapon.

To be effective, the full court press needs to be applied very quickly after a Turnover (when one team loses possession

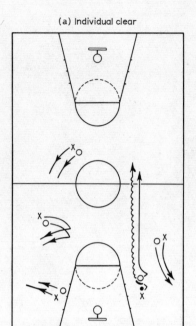

(a) Individual clear

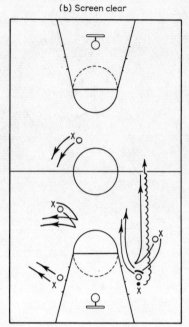

(b) Screen clear

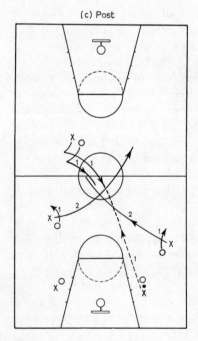

(c) Post

Figure 74

to the other). This is very difficult to do from an interception or rebound, especially when the team gaining possession had been playing zone defence. A pressing player could be great distance from his opponent, and would have to expend much energy to pick up his man, and also be at risk until he had achieved the pickup. Coaches should give very serious consideration to the dangers of applying a press after losing possession against a team playing zone defence.

On the other hand, the press is easier against a man-for-man team, since it would be unusual for odd matches to occur (a defender marking a man who does not mark him). On the turnover, the players should be fairly close to one another. Where the press becomes a real killer is on an out of bounds situation. Here we have a defensive advantage of five players against four, so that one attacker can be 'two-timed' (or double-teamed). Usually the most likely recipient of the throw in is two-timed, and the 5 second rule puts great pressure on the ball handler which often results in a bad error (Fig. 75).

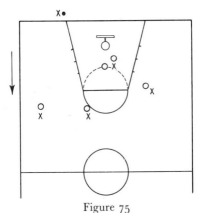

Figure 75

I have always considered it a weakness in the rules which allows a team to violate (perhaps deliberately) by kicking away a pass—thereby gaining a numerical advantage on court. However, such situations should be capitalised, especially straight after a basket has been scored. It is very demoralising to lose a basket, then immediately give away another one against a press. Special plays against these situations will be discussed later.

Three quarter and half court presses are safer to apply, in that the defenders can initially fall back on the turnover, then look for their men. Such tactics tend to be used as methods of pressuring weak ball handlers as they bring the ball up court. Versions are sometimes used where the defenders of the ball handlers apply the press, leaving their team mates to retreat to the shooting area. This method can be most efficient in combining the virtues of both pressing and supporting.

A properly applied press is very physically demanding. This is not necessarily because the defenders have to run much further or faster than attackers, but because the time distance advantage (page 96) of the defenders is lost. Each player has to generate much more power in the shorter time available to him to react to attacker's moves. If his opponent is mobile and aggressive the cumulative effect of this short burst power production can destroy all but the very fittest of players. For this reason, a real press is rarely applied other than in short bursts of a few minutes. In fact, many coaches will bring a completely fresh five on court to apply a killer press, taking them off again after they have achieved (or not) their shock effect!

Support Man-for-Man Defence

I have earlier made the point that it is unusual for a coach to have players all of whom are superior to each of his opponent's five. Therefore, defence has more usually to be

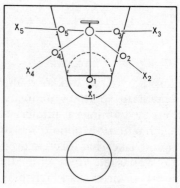

Figure 76

orientated towards giving support to an overloaded player. Within the limits of individual adjustment mentioned on page 101, we should always like the ball handler to be defended closely (Fig. 76). If X_1 should succeed in driving round O_1, then the obvious defenders to give support are O_2 and O_4—depending on which side X_1 goes. So these two retreat from their man back along a line towards the basket. This is called Sagging. The precise distance of the sag will depend on many factors, including their opponents' speed and immediate shooting ability. The other two defenders will sag even further from their men, who are even less likely to perform an immediate shot. Many coaches impose a rule of thumb method on their defenders to gauge sagging distance. A highly specific method is to say 'One stride away for each pass your man is from the ball'. In Figure 76 X_3 is two passes from the ball, so O_3 comes two strides away. A less specific method is to say 'Stand at a distance so that, by the time your man can possibly receive the ball, you can get into a good defensive position on him'. On the whole, I prefer the second method, which allows more scope for individual variation. Needless to say, all my previous remarks on stance and movement in part one apply.

So far, our support has been achieved by movement in one plane only—towards basket. We have seen on page 92 how movement towards the ball can also be effective in hampering passes, and it would also put the defender in a good position to switch to a successful driver. This is called Floating, and is

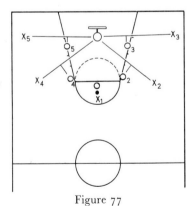

Figure 77

Plate 78 Aldershot Warriors' man-for-man defence. Pearce (Loughborough) has just shot, his defender sags since Pearce is not rebounding. 9 sags from 7. 5 floats from 4, but with a bias to break up court. 11 starts to block out. 14 has sagged, and now blocks out.

illustrated in Figure 77. Each defender's position is shown as a sag along the line to basket and a float at right angles to that line. The support capabilities of that defence have now very much improved.

We are introducing an important idea to our man-for-man defenders, that not only should their movement be related to the movement of their man but also to the movements and

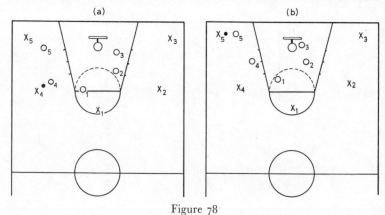

Figure 78

154

subsequent positions of the ball. For instance, if the offence remains stationary while passing the ball from the position shown in Figure 77, the defence may move considerably (Fig. 78).

The defence is achieving a high degree of support, but at the expense of maintaining a matched pattern. This may involve them in some relatively tiring movement around the court, while their opponents stand still. However, only on rare occasions would an offence stand still, since they want to create scoring opportunities. As soon as they begin to move, they make the defenders' job easier. In sagging, the defender has put himself on the inside of a circle. If his opponent moves around the outside of the defence, or cuts through it, the total distance covered by the defender will be less than that by the attacker (Fig. 79).

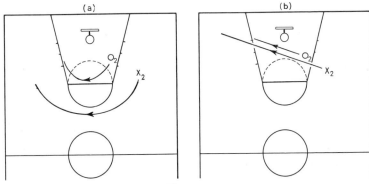

Figure 79

Even though his opponent's changing proximity to the ball will make it necessary for him to adjust his relative distance, the defender can still adequately cover the non ball handler without a tremendous expenditure of energy.

Although the offence will discover that passing and moving against a support man-for-man is relatively easy, driving and convergence plays are not. The driver who tries to get all the way to basket should find himself running into a succession of lines of defence. Beat one—and he will encounter another. Convergences into screens and posts will find that the looseness of the defence facilitates over the top and sifting manoeuvres (page 124). Screen plays off the ball should be

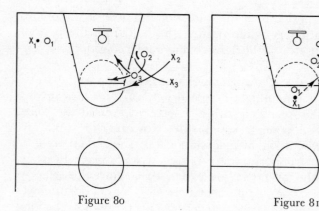

Figure 80   Figure 81

nullified by this looseness, since a hard screen is almost impossible against alert defenders (Fig. 80). Though X_3 sets a screen, O_2 is so far from X_2 that he can just step around the screen without much difficulty. The offence must therefore concentrate on the weak aspects of support man-for-man, that is, the space given to off the ball players. Immediate shots are an important weapon especially if extra time for the shot can be gained by a screen, as in Figure 81. Though this seems just too simple, it is a move which the England team have used with great success recently, forcing defenders to press much more closely. Another move which is becoming increasingly popular in this age of very tall athletic players is the Weakside Backdoor Cut (Fig. 82). Here O_2 may find it difficult to see both his man and the ball, and may merely look alternately at the ball and his man. X_2 waits until O_2 glances away, and then cuts along the baseline for a high lead pass into an immediate shot. In some cases it can be legal for such players to catch the pass above ring level and stuff it straight down through the basket. Most disconcerting!

One other weakness of this type of support defence is the centre. If a really mobile centre forms a closed offence, then he is *always* 'one pass away' from the ball (Fig. 83). His defender cannot afford to sag, but may float towards the ball, thus half- or full-fronting him. As the ball moves around the outside, the half-fronting defender may suddenly find himself hopelessly out of position (Fig. 84). If the defender is half-fronting during this type of manoeuvre, there comes a time when he needs to

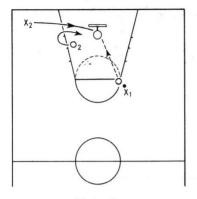

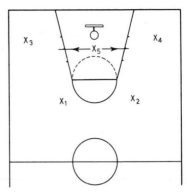

Figure 82   Figure 83

change from one side to the other by moving around the back
of the centre. If the ball can be passed to the centre at this
time he can be free for an obstruction shot.

In making the point that a good centre can be a thorn in
the flesh of a support defence, we should also be aware that
once he gets the ball, the four outside defenders have a duty
to float towards the ball and sag away from their man. The
centre should therefore find himself double or even triple-
teamed by the outside defenders on his side (Fig. 85). These
will very often commit themselves fully to collapsing on the
centre, and can make life very difficult for him. If, however,
he is very cool and tall, he can quickly pass the ball outwards
for a forward or guard to take an immediate shot.

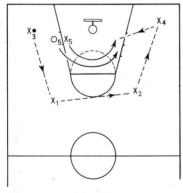

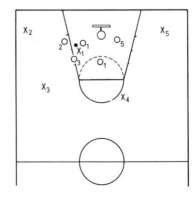

Figure 84   Figure 85

157

Man-for-Man Rebounding

We have earlier seen the point that possessions gained by rebounding are often crucial to the result of a game. Furthermore, we know that defensive rebounding tends to be more successful if the attacking rebounder is blocked out from the ball (page 115). Since the technique of blocking out depends to a large extent on being near to one's opponent, then a defence which achieves this state of affairs will be ideal for blocking out. Certainly it would seem that man-for-man defence would fit the bill, especially a pressing man-for-man. Even a sagging defender should know where his man is, and be able to move more efficiently into his intended path. Moreover, a star offensive rebounder may be cut out from the boards by a pressing defender, who may not even attempt to rebound himself. This play is often used by a defender who is much smaller than his opponent. On the other hand, the offence against man-for-man will often move one of its own players away from the rebounds if they know that the man marking him is a strong rebounder. So, it cuts both ways! On the whole, though, the best defence for blocking out, and thus for rebounding, is man-for-man.

Zone Defence

The reader will have realised from my earlier comments that I consider zone defence to be the least important defence, certainly for use in Britain. Unfortunately, it is the most used defence because it is the easiest defensive form *when played badly*. The idea of getting to a spot on court and just standing there with arms extended like a tree is a very attractive one to the untalented and immobile player. Offences are presented with wide open spaces at ranges of 15 ft plus, from which they can take shots with impunity. Any team with reasonable medium and long range shots can tear such defence to ribbons, and yet the defence makes no changes merely complaining at being forced to play in the same league as the opposing supermen!

My name for such play is 'Non-defence'. I would certainly not call it Zone defence, and any reader who expects a list of magical formations, from which *one* can be selected as suitable for his team to play non defence, is doomed to disappointment.

In spite of its limited applicability in the present scene, hopefully there will come a time when a greater proportion of our clubs can use zone, and I must give it a fair coverage in a comprehensive text such as this. Due to the complexity of the topic, zone defence will therefore occupy more space in the book than any other single aspect—and more space than its present importance warrants.

Zone Patterns

The first principle of defence is to match the pattern of the offence. Man-for-man can achieve this aim by giving each defender the task of standing by an opponent. The construction of a zone, however, puts defenders in their most advantageous court positions, irrespective of the type of opponent they may then be facing. So, the best defensive rebounders can be positioned near to basket, the fastest and most aggressive defender can take the opposing ball handler, etc. Each defender then has an area of prime responsibility, within which he *must* attempt to defend the ball. Figure 86, shows a 1–3–1 and a 2–1–2 zone defensive formation, with shaded areas indicating typical areas of prime responsibility. Theoretically, wherever the ball is within the shooting area, it will then be defended. The great difficulty for the defence

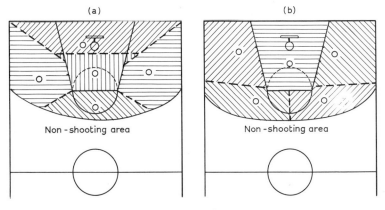

Figure 86

comes when opponents play the ball from positions close to the intersection lines between areas. Defenders can then become confused about their division of duties.

If a method can be devised of selecting a defensive pattern which matches the offensive pattern, such 'borderline confusion' can be minimised. With a poor offensive team, playing a relatively static offence against zone, it is easy to spot their formation and adopt a similar one for the defence. So the coach may take a time out, or merely call to the players, telling them the formation they should adopt. It never ceases to amaze me, the number of teams who will stick to one offensive formation throughout a game, despite it having been nullified by the defensive adaptation.

However, it is not always so easy, and an alert offence may very well change its basic shape quite frequently. In this case, the defence needs a method of adapting to *any* shape. On page 84. I made the point that there are really only two basic formations—open and closed. To this one might add that the quarterback play may be achieved by either one or two guards. Typical offensive formations can then be described as shown.

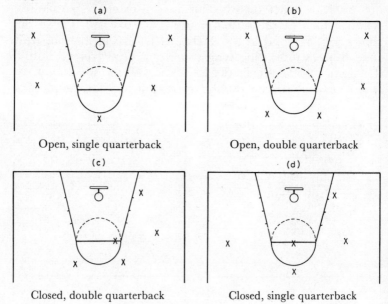

(a)

Open, single quarterback

(b)

Open, double quarterback

(c)

Closed, double quarterback

(d)

Closed, single quarterback

Figure 87

In this case, all the defence has to do is decide on two points—'open or closed', 'single or double quarterback'. Though the actual floor positions of the attackers may vary, they still come within this overall scheme. For instance, a closed-single offence could take any of the precise forms (or others) seen in Figure 88.

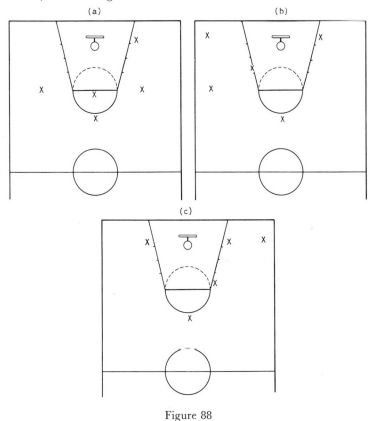

Figure 88

Initially the defence needs to take a 'neutral' formation from which it can easily adapt—perhaps a 1–3–1. Figure 89 shows such a formation, with the player's positions specified. From this neutral position, the first guard decides whether the offence is single or double quarterback. If single then he remains in his basic position. If double, then he moves to one prearranged side. In doing so, his team mates rotate with him,

161

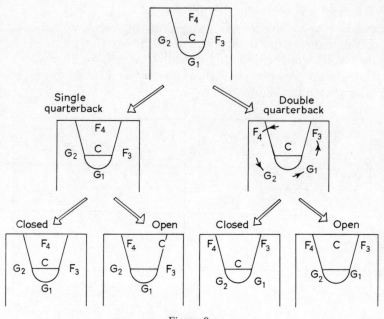

Figure 89

around the centre, rather like spokes on a wheel rotating around the hub. The next decision rests with the centre. If the offence is closed, then he remains where he is. If open, then he retreats to a prearranged side of the basket. Such a system, which can be learned by any reasonable team in a single session, allows for any of the four basic offensive formations shown in Figure 87 to be matched. The precise forms of the basic formation, examples of which were shown in Figure 88, are then catered for by normal rotation of the zone, and sagging and floating principles similar to those used in man-for-man defence.

The reader might be forgiven if he wondered why all this trouble should have been taken to achieve what man-for-man can do quite simply. The *only* reason is to achieve the best floor position for each defender, which is certainly a very worthwhile aim. Where the zone begins to differ fundamentally from man-for-man is in what takes place *from* this pattern matching situation.

Offensive Overload

Since the offence wish to place two attackers in an area defended by one opponent, they must adopt a pattern different to that of the defence. If the patterns are different, then there *must* be overload, the precise location and magnitude of the overload depending upon the coach's assessment of his strengths and opponents' weaknesses. Some commonly used offensive overloads are illustrated in Figure 90.

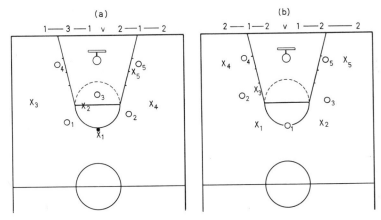

Figure 90

a) O_1 versus $X_1 + X_2 + X_3$ b) O_2 versus $X_1 + X_3 + X_4$

    O_4 ,, $X_2 + X_3$ O_1 ,, $X_1 + X_2 + X_3$

    O_2 ,, $X_1 + X_4$ O_3 ,, $X_2 + X_5$

    O_5 ,, $X_4 + X_5$ O_4 ,, $X_3 + X_4$

The first example shows a closed offence against a closed defence, with overloads being created mainly for medium range or outside shots. The second shows a closed offence against an open defence, providing more opportunities for the offensive centre.

It might be thought that all this is a rather academic exercise, since players do not just stand absolutely still and watch the opposition shoot. True, but if the defence persist in operating from a basic pattern *without* adaption, then continuous passing of the ball around one or two overladen defenders can run them into the ground. As soon as a defender

163

slows down or is less than aggressive, the attacker with the ball should shoot. If the attacker is standing in a position from which he cannot shoot then there is a fundamental error in the offensive set up!

Another commonly used tactic is to put two attackers close together so that one can use the other as a screen over which he can shoot or around which he can drive (Fig. 91).

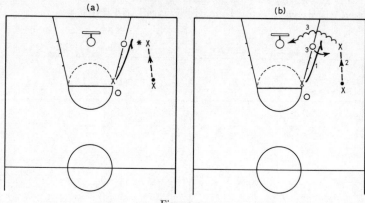

Figure 91

In general though, zone offence is a little more difficult than this because each defender does not limit himself to an actual floor area (bounded by imaginary or real lines). If the pattern of the defence is determined by the offensive pattern, *then a defender will base his area upon the attacker who is nearest him after the pattern match.* In this case, every defender has a 'man' to defend, this man being the one with whom he has been matched by the defensive adaption. That man can be considered as the focal point of the defender's area, and if the offence has created an overload, it does so at the expense of balancing its power over the whole shooting area. *Therefore, there will be a part of the shooting area which is not covered by a defender.* Figure 92 shows an extreme example of such a situation. Just under one half of the shooting area is vacant. The areas of O_3, O_4 and O_5, if centred on X_3, X_4 and X_5 respectively, provide a great deal of overlap—which is extremely necessary in a situation such as this. In fact, one might look for another definition of 'shooting area' at this stage in our development—that is 'the area from which shots

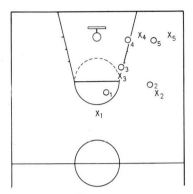

Figure 92

are likely'. Then we can more easily understand the defenders' function in the zone, because it remains one of subdividing the shooting area (as now re-defined) between the five defenders.

Even now, the reader might reiterate his earlier comment that it has taken an awful lot of fuss and bother to create a defence which man-for-man could have done very easily. Indeed, against a very good defence, it is difficult to tell whether man-for-man or zone is being used. I still take it as a great compliment to overhear opponents saying 'What a great man-for-man that was!'—when we had been playing zone!

At this point we can see the second major difference between the defences emerging. In an overload situation, a defender still has a prime responsibility to stop the ball handler in his area from shooting. The fact that the shooter might not be the man against whom he is 'pattern matched' and upon whom his defensive area has been based is to a great

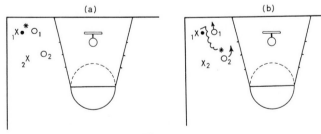

Figure 93

165

extent irrelevant. Figure 93 has two attackers, both within the areas of *both* defenders. Situation (a), where X_1 shoots, is obviously O_1's responsibility, but in (b) where O_1 has been faked out, the shooter is still within O_2's area, and should be checked by him. This manoeuvre looks in fact like a switch, but cannot strictly be defined as such because the ball handler was at this stage the responsibility of *both* defenders.

Against such good zone defences, it is not much use to stand and pass, or even to converge and pass, since the support afforded by zone principles is considerable. On the other hand, divergence with player mobility can be extremely effective. We have already seen how the defence will adapt by rotation, with the proviso that 'spokes of the wheel cannot overtake one another'. Defenders pass moving players on from one to the other, as illustrated in Figure 94. This again looks like a switch

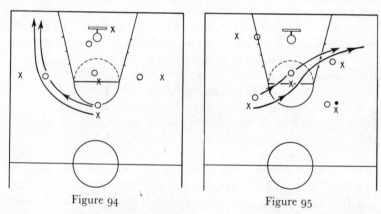

Figure 94   Figure 95

but isn't! Even if a diagonal cut is made (Fig. 95) the spoke of the defensive wheel doesn't overtake the 'hub'—though the hub is displaced somewhat, the wheel is already starting to buckle. The main benefit of zone defence being to have players occupying their most advantageous positions, to have a guard coping with a pivot may not be considered efficient. If at the same time the offensive centre moves out (Fig. 96), the adjustments of three defenders could easily lead to error, especially if they concern the ball handler's defender. We might be forgiven for abandoning ship at this point, retreating to man-for-man with sighs of relief. But if we consider that these

166

Figure 96

defensive movements are very similar to the automatic switching described on page 127, we can see how a well prepared team could manage the moves with little energy expenditure and yet maintain a very effective blanket defence.

I still believe, personally, that the individual overload is a major problem even with the best of zone defences. There must be a weak link in most zones. Overload this and even a good defence must commit itself to support, creating weaknesses in other parts of the defence. It is easier for individual defenders to cope with these problems if they have *an opponent* to act as a cue for their situation assessment. *Areas* are such nebulous things in basketball!

Zone Press

This is a terribly physically demanding weapon, which can win or lose games in dramatic fashion. To a great extent a coach using Zone Press is gambling against the odds, and can often come badly unstuck. Whereas in man-for-man press, once the ball is in play each attacker is marked by a defender, a zone press will put two defenders against an attacker—a 'defensive overload' in fact. Quite obviously, this leaves the remainder of the *defence* overladen, but if the ball can be kept within the *defensive overload* the ball handler can often be pressurised into errors or held ball situations (Fig. 97).

To keep the ball in the *defensive* overload area, a pass into the *offensive* overload area must be prevented. There are the

167

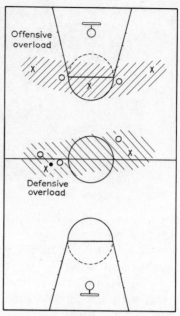

Figure 97

usual two aspects to this pass prevention. First, the passer must be hampered from releasing the ball—at least from releasing it in a dangerous direction. Second, the other defenders must be positioned so that they can intercept dangerous passes.

The first task can be achieved if the press is put on very quickly, either as soon as the ball handler receives the ball (which might mean a full court press), or if the ball handler is surprised by a sudden press imposed from a 'normal' zone defence position. The second aspect, that is the cutting off of the pass, is made from a floating defence. The distance over which the ball must be thrown can allow an alert defender time for interception.

The 'ifs and buts' in this situation give the clue about offensive methods against the zone press. Firstly, the ball handler should pass the ball before the two defenders have reached him (or, if he is already double teamed, he should not be given the ball). Secondly, the offensive overload should diverge, the free man then cutting into a high post

168

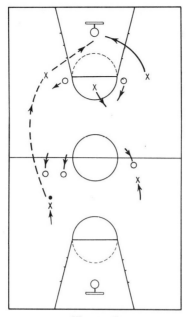

Figure 98

position or going backdoor to the basket (Fig. 98). It is vital for the offence, once having passed the ball forward, *not to cut towards basket*, since they would then be nullifying the offensive overload. Conversely, the defence must motor back very quickly to help against the overload!

It is possible that one quarterback can make a pass to another when opposed by the 3 v 2 overload of our example. In this case, not only will the receiver of the pass be pressed by his defender, but the nearer of the other two defenders will cross as quickly as possible to make it a double team (Fig. 99), and so on, to and fro for as long as is necessary.

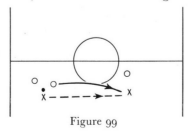

Figure 99

Some coaches assign actual floor areas to individual defenders in zone press, but in my opinion such tactics will only succeed against a poor offence. When pressing a competent team, it is much more successful to base the zones upon the position of the attackers, as a natural extension of normal zone methods. Less frequently, a zone press is applied by two defenders against a single quarterback, which seems peculiar since the element of risk is much smaller (Fig. 100). In my own experience as a quarterback I know that such 2 v 1 presses have caused me the most trouble, since it can be difficult to spot a team mate for a pass before the press is jammed on.

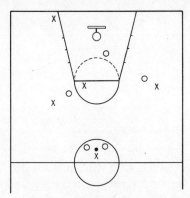

Figure 100

Ken Johnson, the Scottish coach, was a devotee of zone press, and certainly stole a close international match from Wales in 1967 by bottling me up with a two man press.

It is a disturbing feature of many teams, including some quite talented outfits, that they will gradually allow a game to slip away from them, or fail to pull back a few point deficit at the end of a game, without attempting a radical tactical change. Admittedly, they stand a chance of losing by a greater margin, but on the other hand an aggressively applied zone or man-for-man press can sometimes turn the tide. Even if it only works once in five or six games—it is worthwhile.

Perhaps an even more disturbing feature, particularly in British basketball, is the lack of method and self control of a team facing a press. My own team has been trained to combat the press, using a system which very rarely fails. However, we have lost one international match this season where we out-scored the opposition for 36 minutes, but lost a quick ten points against a man-for-man press over the other 4 minutes. It was not that the players didn't know *what* to do, or did not have the playing ability to do it. It was just that the surprise and ferocity of the press knocked them off balance, and they lost their self control temporarily. That's the way to press!

Combination Defence

Our consideration of the two basic defensive forms has shown us many of the benefits of each system, many of the defects which arise when the system is used by incompetent players, and some defects which are inherent in the systems them-selves. Theoretically, if we could take those parts of each system which worked well for our team, leaving out that which was defective, an amalgamation of these successful parts might give us an overall efficiency in defence which might otherwise be unattainable. This might well produce a hybrid defence which looked odd, but which was tailor-made and successful in use. Such are called Combination Defences.

Since 1962 when I first coached internationally I have always included combination defences in my teams' reper-toires. Our national domestic standard is so low, by comparison with many of the nations we oppose, that we have to make up in fitness, morale and tactics much of what we lack in ability. Tailormade combination defences have very often given me surprising victories over much more fancied opponents.

There tend to be two commonly used combinations—a four man zone with one chaser, and a triangle zone with two chasers.

Box (or Diamond) and One

Where there is one outstanding offensive star, the best defender is assigned to him on a man-for-man basis, with instructions to the other defenders that the star attacker is also their responsibility when in their area. If, therefore, he happens to get the ball, he should immediately be opposed by two men.

This, naturally, involves some weakness since it is a 2 v 1 press, leaving at least one attacker relatively free. Sometimes, against a team with a very good player, it is worth it.

The four zone defenders will form an open defence, and rotate in the normal fashion to adapt to offensive manoeuvres. Tradition has called the zone a box when it is 2–2, and a Diamond when it is 1–2–1. It doesn't really matter what name is used, as long as the term chosen does not exclude the defence from passing into one through the other formation!

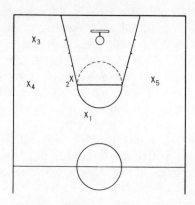

Figure 101

Problems can be caused by an offence which uses a centre player and a heavy overload. If X_5 is the offensive star, then he has virtually a clear play against his chaser O_5. If X_1 were the star, then a drive off X_2 as a post would result in O_2 and O_1 double teaming him, leaving X_2 free. Another common move is for the star to play centre, which makes the defence into virtually a normal closed zone. However, provided the offence is not a particularly mobile one, the zone players can provide a great deal of support and also individual positional strength, while the chaser worries the star. The coach may, or may not, allow switching if the chaser becomes screened out— depending on the strength of the star. If there is a switch, the chaser becomes a zone player, and the 'switcher' becomes chaser!

Triangle and Two

This is a more formal subdivision of duties, where one part of the shooting area is defended on zone principles by the triangle of three players, and the other part covered by man-for-man. The most common form of 3–2 combination uses the strong rebounding triangle of a zone defence (either 2–1–2 or 2–2–1), with the aggressive man-for-man defence of outside shots (Fig. 102). Here X_3, X_4 and X_5 form the triangle, with slightly enlarged areas which still depend upon the positions of O_3, O_4, O_5. The normal rotation rules of zone apply in this triangle. X_1 and X_2 play a normal aggressive man-for-man defence.

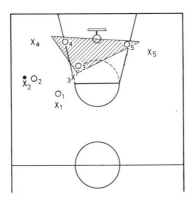

Figure 102

In a triangle and two defence switching is much more common place, not only between the two chasers, but also between chaser and zoner. A switch back to original jobs is usually called for as soon as the danger is over.

A fairly common move against the combination is to bring one of the deep forwards outside and against such formations the triangle normally should invert itself (Fig. 103). Since only three players are concerned in the zone adaptions, it is possible to develop a very high degree of co-ordination between them. From the basic position (usually a 1–2) the front line defender (sometimes called the Point) will float across court to whichever side is overladen by the offensive three, this overload being his cue to initiate the move (Fig. 104).

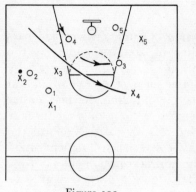
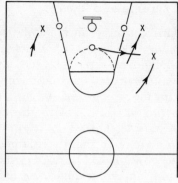

Figure 103   Figure 104

In a situation where the offensive big men are very mobile and yet the attacking guards relatively easy to cope with, the whole combination can be inverted (Fig. 105). Here the triangle is formed by O_3, O_4 and O_5, who once again must be prepared to shift backwards if the offence decide to play deep. X_1 and X_2 are played man-for-man, both of them being pressed and probably fronted as they cut towards the ball. The danger of this defence is that any outside attacker who can go backdoor on his man may get completely clear under the basket, with little chance of running into defensive support from the big man, who are pressing. This is especially the case on rebounds if a triangle defender cannot block out adequately. This particular combination is not used frequently enough in these days of very athletic big men. It could pay big dividends.

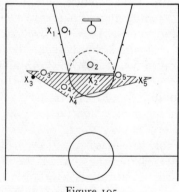

Figure 105

One of the most enjoyable things about playing combination defence is to hear one's opponents calling out conflicting instructions about the nature of the defence. I have actually witnessed a flaming great row amongst the playing five and coach of opponents during an early time out when we have used combination. Even at the end of the game they were still unsure, and I think that a riot might well have ensued if they hadn't happened to have beaten us! I consoled myself (and the team) by pointing out that it had been a relatively narrow defeat by comparison with previous wide margins. Next time we would win—and we very well may!

Opposing a good combination defence is a very difficult job. Each aspect of the combination, considered singly, is very strong. The chasers have a relatively simple task to bottle up the opposing ball handlers; the zone players have easier group pattern adaptations to perform since there are fewer players involved. An attacking system which merely undertakes a straight forward confrontation with each section is unlikely to prove successful. For instance, against a box and one the star attacker stands less chance of scoring if he merely tries to beat his man on 1 v 1 principles; against a 2 and 3 combination the attacking quarterbacks stand very little chance of achieving a successful screen (or pick and roll) drive.

The offence should in fact, against a *good* combination, try to cause a single- or multi-switching situation *between* the two sections of defence. Figure 106a shows a pick and roll play on the weak side of the zone. Since the zone defender O_1 will normally not press his man, the attacking ball handler is free for an immediate shot for a considerable time after accepting the screen. If the defensive switch is successful, the pick and roll should give the screening attacker an immediate shot (Fig. 106b) unless the strong side defenders have sagged right across. In this case, O_2 who will be performing a defensive roll to complete the defensive switch, *and thus be defending on zone principles,* will be badly out of position whichever way he goes. O_4 will defend X_1, being in his zone with the ball, leaving O_5 to face two attackers. A quick pass to either X_4 or X_5 gives an immediate shooting opportunity because O_2, even if he is not totally confused and rooted to the spot, cannot cover the ground sufficiently quickly to help

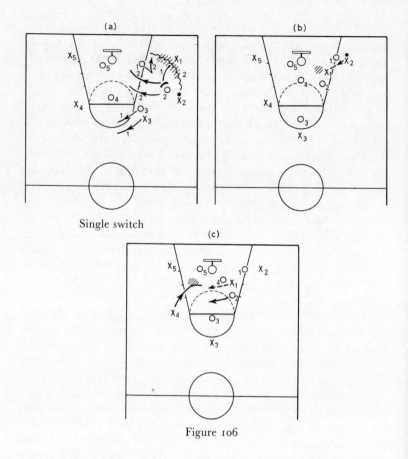

(a)

(b)

Single switch

(c)

Figure 106

out on the opposite side of the court from where he started
(Fig. 106c).

Offensive moves such as these are complex in description,
but relatively simple in operation. A pick and roll is all that is
required, with the ball always being passed to a free man.
The defensive adjustments, though fairly simple in description,
involve individual defenders in making very quick adjustments
from man-for-man principles to zone, and perhaps also in
covering large areas of court in coping with defensive formation changes. It needs a very good team defence to cope with
such demands.

176

Mobility

We have already seen enough to become convinced that mobility is necessary on both offence and defence, and that mobility applies to both men and ball. The defence should always move towards the ball, and space for attackers is created when there is relative divergence between attacker and defender. In this case *attacking space is created when the ball moves away from the attacker.* Figure 107 shows defender O_5 moving further away from X_5 as the ball moves away. Ball mobility has created attacking space. If the ball is mobile enough, that is moving far enough and fast enough, defenders can be forced to slow down by fatigue, laziness or non-co-ordination, therefore adding time and space in which an attacker can receive the ball and shoot.

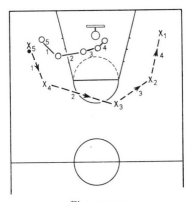

Figure 107

When I read that last paragraph through again, I get the nagging suspicion that I have merely said something very obvious and made it sound like the secret of life! Of course it's obvious—on paper; but in games, in actual play, how rarely do we see a team who do achieve this kind of ball mobility. The cynic might say 'How rarely do we see a defence which will move sufficiently to make ball mobility necessary'! Possibly so, but I am not concerned with 'non-defence', and any basketballer who has had sufficient interest to remain with me so far will realise that almost any method of offence can beat a non-defence.

177

Figure 107 illustrated ball mobility around the outside of the defence, which generally has to be persisted with for a considerable number of passes before achieving a 'space-time' shooting opportunity. Most offences don't have the patience to persist. On the other hand, Figure 108 illustrates how ball mobility which penetrates the defence can cause it to collapse rather like a pricked balloon. If the ball mobility is maintained by an immediate pass back out of the defence, the outside attackers have a chance for an immediate shot. A pass to the strong side is obviously easiest to make (to X_4 and X_2), but the weak side defenders will probably have sagged further—forgetting that their men are only one pass away from the ball—so that an immediate pass to X_1 or X_3 can be even more effective.

Mobility of the ball which attempts penetration of the defence can be much more effective than external mobility, but is much more susceptible to interception and forced errors. For this reason, the offensive centre needs to be a man who is easy to hit with the ball, generally a mobile tall man taking and giving high plane passes.

There are very important differences between the ball and man in terms of mobility (mentioned on pages 34 and 79). Amongst the most important is that there is a choice of men to fill any court position—whereas there is only one ball. Player mobility is therefore not only restricted by speed and space, but also by the specific nature of each player and the

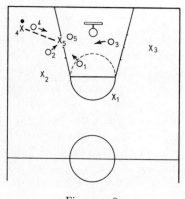

Figure 108

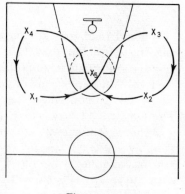

Figure 109

most efficient court areas he should occupy. It is not enough for a coach to use player mobility to create a certain shooting position if the player with the ball has not the ability (physical or otherwise) to capitalise on that position.

Player mobility, then, tends to be restricted by player function. If I may repeat an earlier diagram (Fig. 109) we can see one form of player mobility which tends to repeat a certain pattern on court. At that stage (page 131) we could merely be concerned with pattern, but we can now see that X_1, for instance, might be a very small ball handling genius who likes to operate on the left hand side of court. It would take four complete team shifts before he found himself back in his most effective floor area. *En route*, he would have played in two positions for which he was completely unsuited!

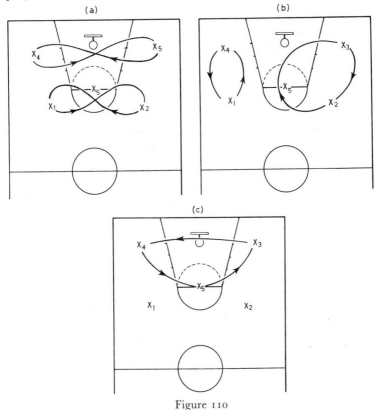

Figure 110

At least some of these problems can be avoided by involving only two players (Fig. 110a and b) or three (Fig. 110c) in any movement pattern. The precise form and specific player involvement in this movement depends to a great extent upon the principle of keeping players in their most effective areas, apart from other normal tactical considerations.

Obviously, since player mobility aims to create scoring opportunities, any player must be moving in such a way that he can best play the ball if it comes to him. Contrast the two cutting players starting from similar positions in Figure 111. X_2 cuts in such a way that after receiving a hand off pass from X_5 he has to dribble and shoot *whilst* also swerving to the right and travelling laterally to the basket. On the other hand, X_1 completes his directional change before taking the ball, and has a simpler direct route to the basket. The total distance run by each cutter is approximately the same.

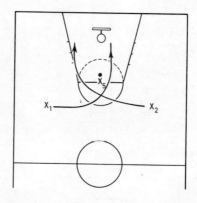

Figure 111

If we extend this idea to complete team function, Figure 112 (a and b) illustrates the difference on a simple rotation play of the direction of movement relative to the ball.

It is especially important also to consider the tactical implications of mobility offence in convergent plays against man-for-man (Fig. 113). Here, the easiest screen for X_4 to set is one which gives X_5 a left handed dribble into an area of defensive support—not so good if he is predominantly right handed! However, the screen and roll would give X_4 a right

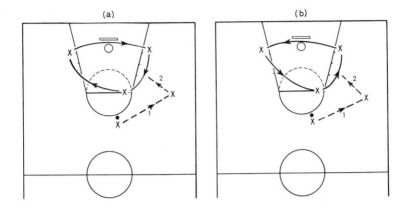

Figure 112

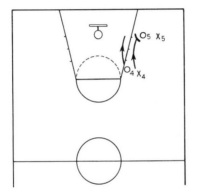

Figure 113

handed dribble into a weak defensive area. Against a switching team, such a screen would be useful. Against a non-switching team, the screen would be better set the other side.

Defensive Balance

'The best laid schemes o' mice an' men gang aft a-gley'—the great Robbie Burns would obviously have been an excellent basketball coach! The appreciation that our best basketball players are still liable to human error forces the intelligent coach to plan for the sudden turnover. His 'best laid' offensive plan may rely to a great extent on player mobility, but it should be a cardinal rule that his defensive balance must be maintained. Whether he decides on one, two, or even three guards, that number *and* their relative positions must be maintained during offensive mobility.

In the simplest case, where defensive balance is maintained by one quarterback (Fig. 114), an opportunity for him to drive to basket might be too good to ignore. If, however, he loses possession *en route*, either from a fumble or a tackle, it is easy for him and his team mates to be outnumbered in the rush to the other end of the court! It is vital, therefore, that as X_1 moves in, some other attacker moves out (such as X_2, X_3 or X_5).

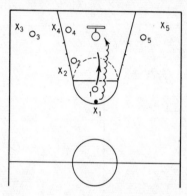

Figure 114   Figure 115

It may be that the driving opportunity was created by a screen, in which case defensive balance is achieved if the screener X_5 remains out. If, however, X_5 is to pick and roll, then X_2 or X_3 must come back out. My own instructions usually are that I *never* want a pick and roll from a screen set for a quarterback.

Of course, it is so difficult for an aggressive offence to maintain defensive balance. We saw earlier in our consideration of zone press how two areas of overload can arise, one favouring the offence, the other the defence (page 167). Since all offence is constructed on the principle of overload, it *automatically* becomes overladen itself in one area when it overloads the defence in another. Once again, the offence wants to get the ball into the offensive overload area (Fig. 116),

182

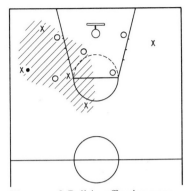

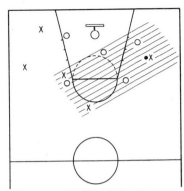

Figure 116 Ball in offensive overload area

Figure 117 Ball in defensive overload area

whereas the defence would like the ball to be in the defensive
overload area, *particularly if it can achieve a turnover in that area*
(Fig. 117).

In almost all cases, the defence tries to prevent offensive
overload, thus nullifying its own possible advantage of
defensive overload. But if the offence has been successful the
defence, without even trying, achieves an overload of its own
which might prove of great value on a quick turnover.
Furthermore, there are special occasions when a defence
might deliberately allow an offensive (numerical) overload to
be countered by a defensive (ability) overload—especially

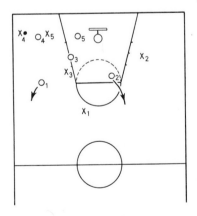

Figure 118

183

when a shot has been taken. Knowing that there is a high probability of the defence obtaining possession by virtue of its superior interception or rebounding ability, one or two defenders more or less surreptitiously create an overload against their opponents' defensive balance (Fig. 118). By encouraging X_4 to shoot, or aggressively intercepting the ball, the defenders hope to be able to obtain possession of the ball *and* pass it to the new overload situation created by O_1 and O_2. Such moves are generally termed 'Stealaway Breaks', and demand a very strong rear defence combined with an organised 'offensive balance'.

Fast Break

On page 133 I investigated the various possibilities which arose from the 'firstest with the mostest' principle. If we combine these possibilities with the defensive overload situations of the previous paragraphs, designed to achieve a fast turnover, we have a total system of getting the ball and scoring which goes under the general heading of fast break. The organisation of our defence achieves the initial securing of possession *and* an overload—the final approach organisation achieves productive shooting opportunities.

There are many teams, probably the majority of good teams, for whom fast break is the main weapon of offence—if not the main, certainly the first. Their play is usually very exciting to watch, and their players are fit and mobile athletes in the wider sense of the word. Inherent in their play, either conscious or unconsciously, is an appreciation of the principles of Transposition. This can be defined as 'efficient movement from one end of the court to another', and involves the whole team as well as the individual. Let us consider a comparison in Figure 119 (a, b and c) between inefficient and efficient transposition.

Obviously c is desirable in terms of effort and speed, but it requires that players obey these principles, irrespective of their defensive position when the turnover occurs. If a player finishes up on the right hand side of the court at the turnover, then he proceeds to the right or the centre of the court at the other end—he does not cross over to the left. This instruction

(a)

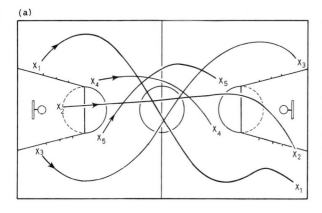

An extremely inefficient transposition, which achieves an efficient offensive position.

(b)

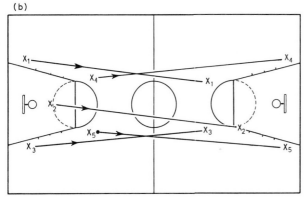

A very efficient transposition, with an inefficient offensive player development.

(c)

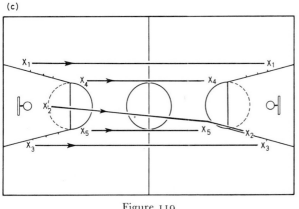

An example of good transposition, using the shortest distance between two points, no diagonal runs, and good player development.

Figure 119

185

has to be modified if the defensive formation is essentially different from the desired offensive formation; but certainly on the fast break transposition must take precedence over the positional demands of a 'set' offence. Should the fast break fail, then players may adjust their offensive positions with perhaps a lesser sense of urgency.

Using these three facets (ball acquisition, transposition and shot), let us construct a more or less formal fast break. The finer points of detail and technique have been covered in relevant earlier sections, we are now concerned with overall plan.

As an example we shall suppose the break to be composed of two waves, three men in the first and two in the second. Since we have to acquire the ball, we would normally expect three of our players to *position themselves* ready for a defensive rebound (involving blocking out and triangulation—Fig. 120). After the ball has rebounded, the defensive rebounders know

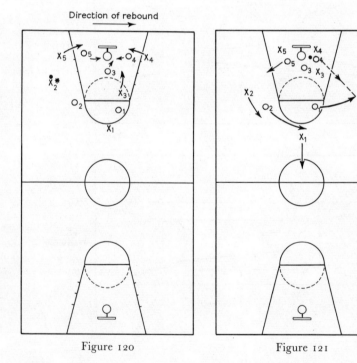

Figure 120   Figure 121

which direction the ball is going, and the two towards whom the ball is going actually attempt the catch. If X_2 has shot, then it is most likely that O_4 and O_3 will go for the ball. O_1, O_2 and O_5 take the ball's rebound direction as a signal and form the first wave of the fast break, filling up three lanes by O_1 and O_2 moving in the same direction as the ball and O_5 moving away from it.

The ball having been caught, say by O_4, he then passes to O_1 (Fig. 121). This pass (the Outlet Pass) is vital to the success of the break. It must be made quickly and safely, helped by O_1's lateral cut to the sideline taking him away from the defender X_1.

If the ball can safely be passed to O_2, who is ahead of the ball, Figure 122 (a and b) shows the first wave in a three lane, ball ahead centre fast break, with a three on two overload. O_2 being ahead, dribbles until forced to stop, but *does not leave his lane*.

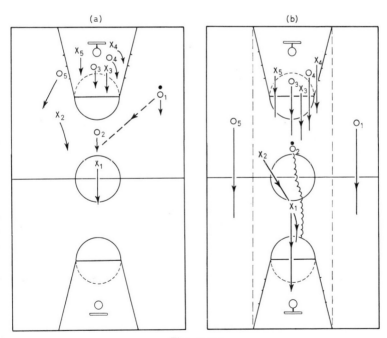

Figure 122

Plate 79 The fast break starts. Gerry Howgill catches and passes in mid air to Gary Brown, already making his way to the side, who then passes to Thomas in the middle.

When O_2, forced to stop by a defender committing himself, passes to O_1 after faking to O_5, O_1 goes in immediately for a shot (Fig. 123). Meanwhile, the second wave of O_3 and O_4 have followed through very powerfully, selected a path to basket and automatically gone in for the rebound. They must *expect* a rebound, even though it may not occur. If they get the ball, they shoot immediately, and one of the most impressive sights in modern basketball is of a second wave big man catching the ball on its way up from the ring and stuffing it straight back down through the basket!

Of course, the first wave may not be able to get a shot off, in which case the man with the ball should pivot away from the basket to set up a post position. He can then pass off to the second wave as they thunder past him! It is vitally important to remember defensive balance principles as the second wave becomes involved at the finish of the fast break. The first wave *must* bring one or two players back out beyond the 'D', not only having a safety effect, but also clearing out to make room for the incoming big men.

If we join all three aspects (and diagrams) together, we have a total picture of the fast break which looks something like this (Fig. 124). I should stress that this is merely one, highly formal, example of a fast break. There are many other formal methods, and an infinite number of informal ones.

A favourite saying of many good coaches is that 'fast break

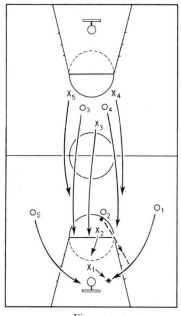
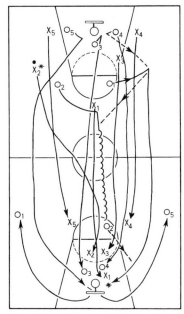

Figure 123   Figure 124

is not so much a method of play, as an attitude of mind'. The fast breaking team is an alert, aggressive, exuberant group of demons, able to demoralise the opposition with fantastic bursts of high scoring, or to break opponents' hearts by scoring straight away after a hardworked basket has been scored against them. Such calculated ferocity, especially when allied with a full blooded pressing defence, has given me some of my most enjoyable games in top class basketball. When you come out of a game like that—you know you've been playing!

Patterns and Plays

The reader will already be aware of my feelings about stereotyped team play (page 119), and yet, as we have delved deeper into the ramifications of team offence it has become obvious that a certain amount of organisation is necessary if a team is to achieve peak efficiency. Once again, the question is 'how much is enough?' Basketball has its fashions, and though the length of a player's trunks doesn't vary quite so alarmingly as young ladies' hemlines, there has certainly been a long history of fluctuations between 'set' and 'free' play.

For most of the game's history, America has set the fashion, since the game was invented in the States, and has always been played most successfully there—if success is measured in terms of technical ability and winning championships. In recent years, other nations have approached more nearly to the Americans' standard, and have created playing fashions of their own, adapted to the particular needs of those nations. This fluctuation and local variation has produced a climate not dissimilar to ladies' fashions, where virtually 'anything goes'. 'If it suits you—wear it' applies to plays as well as clothes!

Unfortunately, too many coaches follow fashions blindly, ending up with entirely unsuitable appearances, and unhappy and unsuccessful existences! A coach *must* examine his own team profile before deciding the degree to which he will use set plays. But what are his guidelines in coming to a decision?

Let us start with the hypothesis that a team will be successful on offence if it overloads the defence in a high probability scoring area. To do this it needs to have methods of putting players and ball in certain positions, to make movements of one or more players and the ball at certain specific times, and to predict the movements of the defence and interfere with them (and to prevent the defence from doing likewise). The first of these points is in fact the achieving of a pattern on offence. Very few coaches would disagree with premise that team offence (with the occasional exception of fastbreak) should start from some pattern or other.

The second point is where the greatest difficulty occurs. For one player to move with the ball from a pattern position is easy. For two people to achieve the same thing in co-ordination is more difficult—and so on through three, four, then to five people. The more complex the co-ordination required, the more necessary is it to restrict the optional elements facing each player. For example, if a coach wanted a clear play for X_1, starting from a closed offence, he could say 'on the signal, I want each of you to see where X_1 is, then choose some place away from him and run to it'; or he could say 'X_1 will have the ball in the "D". On the signal X_2 and

X_3 run to the left hand side line, X_4 and X_5 run to the right hand sideline'. The second of these is more of a set play than the first—and more likely to succeed in terms of clearing out the *attackers*. Each player has only one option, and on the signal—he performs that task. But, and it's a big 'but', since the defence is trying to predict the offence's moves, such a play would be too obvious and each defender would sag off his own man, so that it would only be the attackers who had cleared, and not the defenders.

If the set play can be so complex, or so well disguised, as to be undetectable by the defence, then it can obviously provide enhanced scoring opportunities. However, the achievement of such a complex play would be very difficult indeed, and a team would certainly need to have several such plays in order to foil an intelligent coaching and scouting system. It may take months to train a team to use a complex set play—it only takes minutes for an opposing coach to take a note of the play, and to devise a huge spanner to throw into the works!

There is no general answer to the problem of using set plays, and coaches only really vary in the *degree* to which they use them, and the rigidity of option restriction within the play. If the pros and cons are listed it becomes even more obvious that there can be no hard and fast decisions.

Advantages	*Disadvantages*
Uses individual players most efficiently	Restricts a player in using his own initiative
Facilitates good transposition	Difficult to learn and co-ordinate
Easy to predict defensive movements	Difficult to disguise movements against an alert defence
Calming influence in moments of stress	Vulnerable if the play breaks down
Prevents rushing the play against a set defence	Occasionally ignores profitable shooting opportunities
Good morale booster if the play is run successfully	Bad for morale if play fails

Advantages	*Disadvantages*
Excellent in predictable situations (eg. jump ball, out of bounds, free throw)	Poor against unpredictable defences and unforeseen circumstances.

One could go on adding and subtracting, but the probable upshot of it all would be a compromise based upon the specific demands of each team's situation. The majority of good teams these days:

1. Start their set offence from a pattern.
2. Initiate the moves with some sort of signal.
3. Go through a fairly simple player movement routine, involving few players, perhaps only one.
4. Provide many different shooting options during the play.
5. Allow scope for individual acceptance of any option, or of any other opportunity which might arise.

I should like to give a fairly detailed picture of two typical plays now. The first is a set play against zone defence which provides many options for several players. The play was first shown to me by George Wilkinson, who used it when coaching the Air Force team of which I was a member. I have since used it with great success with my own club team, Loughborough All Stars. Figure 125a shows a starting position for the play, and the first move, being a pass from X_1 to X_3 followed by a cut around the back, with X_2 shifting slightly. O_3 moves towards X_3, O_2 drops back and O_1 may or may not follow X_1 towards X_3. If X_3 is clear, he shoots. If not, he fakes to shoot, ensuring that O_3 comes closer. Meanwhile X_1 continues into the corner. At any stage X_3 can give X_1 the ball if he is free for an immediate shot. If X_1 is not free, the second phase (b) is for the ball to be passed from X_3 to X_2 at the same time as X_1 cuts under the basket. If X_2 is free, he shoots. Sometimes O_1 and O_3 become confused, thus allowing X_1 to get free under the basket, in which case X_2 passes high plane to X_1, who shoots. If O_5 sags, X_2 passes to X_5, who shoots. If the defence is still 'on the ball' (c), X_2 passes to X_4 at the same time as X_1 continues his cut to the opposite corner.

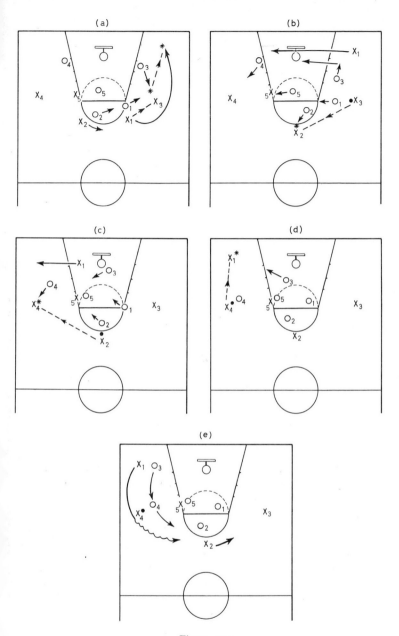

Figure 125

If X_4 is free, he shoots. If not, he fakes to ensure that O_4 comes to him, and passes to X_1 (d), who by now is almost invariably free for an immediate jump shot since there aren't many 'O_3 defenders' who would be mobile enough to keep with him. This is usually the best shooting opportunity. Sometimes O_5 will be alert to the danger, in which case his sag and float leaves X_5 clear for a pass and shot. Very occasionally O_3 does keep up with X_1, in which case (e) X_1 cuts around behind X_4, taking a hand off pass *en route*, and arriving back in the original 2–3 formation (leaving O_3 in a quandry). *From there the whole play can be repeated—on either the original or the opposite side.* A very high degree of defensive adaptation is required to cope with this form of offence; sooner or later, someone becomes confused, makes an error, and the shot is on.

And yet, this fairly complex looking play, with bags of shooting opportunities, involves only one player moving and is relatively simple to operate. The starting signal is merely X_1 beginning his original cut around X_3. Each player has several options, all except the centre get a regular feel of the ball, defensive balance is maintained, and at least two attackers (X_1 and X_5) are ready to cut for a rebound at any time. The offensive manoeuvres capitalise on the zone defence's weakness against rapidly interchanging players, particularly in that the defence's attention (being zone) is focussed to a great extent on the ball.

The second of these two 'typical' plays is designed for use against man-for-man defences. I devised it originally for the England team, and it formed a major part of our offence over the years 1968/71. When I first took over the England team, their average score on offence was 44 points per game. At the time of writing, their average over the last 14 games has been 92 points per game! Since representative teams in Britain have very few opportunities for team training, set plays have to be such that they can be very quickly and easily learned. This man-for-man play is extremely flexible, and really demands combined play from different *pairs* of players, rather than the whole team. The starting pattern is shown in Figure 126. From there, any two adjoining players around the 'horseshoe' can perform the standard offensive manoeuvres

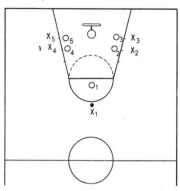

Figure 126

described in pages 122 and 129. This includes pairs involving X_1 as one of the players, with the proviso that he should not be involved in a pick and roll (page 182). Figure 127 shows examples of moves which can ensue.

When one considers that for each of these situations there are several options leading to a shot, and that the opportunities are created both sides of the defence, there are obviously very many possible combinations from this play. It is particularly suited to teams having mobile big men and a talented quarterback, and of course forwards and centres can interchange positions at will, without altering the set up. In the specific case of England, I give them basic instructions about what they can and cannot do from the pattern:

1. The offence must always balance, two on each side and a quarterback. Players, once having set up, must not cross to the other side. If they cut into the middle, they must return to their original side if the attempt is abortive.
2. Movement must be continuous, all players except the quarterback must be continually setting and accepting screens, until the ball can be passed into a good offensive situation.
3. At the time of a shot, players moving towards the basket must continue in for the rebound, all other players must fall back for defensive balance.

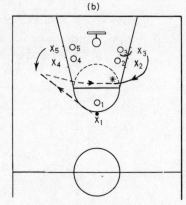

(a)

Screen off the ball, freeing X$_5$ for an immediate jump shot. (NB Once X$_5$ has the ball, any of the previously mentioned two man plays can be used)

(b)

X$_5$ accepts screen, receives pass. X$_3$ has become similarly free and cuts to receive pass from X$_5$, for an immediate shot.

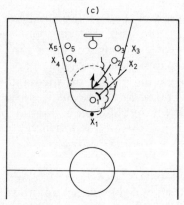

(c)

X$_1$ accepts screen from X$_2$, driving as far as he can before shooting, or passing off to X$_3$ if O$_3$ switches.

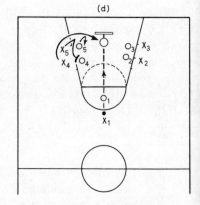

(d)

Backdoor cut by X$_4$, off a screen by X$_5$. X$_1$ passes high plane for X$_4$ to take an immediate shot. This option works infrequently—but is useful if the defence is prepared to press to a considerable distance from basket.

Figure 127

4. The first men down court during transposition select which side they want, the others then fill up the vacant spots.

5. Any player in a medium range shooting position with the ball *must shoot*. Interpassing in the key is dangerous in such cramped situations.

The reader will appreciate that this is a very free approach from a pattern—hardly a set play at all. It contrasts strongly with the more formal zone play, and illustrates the increase in scoring opportunities which arises when players have a greater number of options to choose from. In addition, the defence find it much more difficult to predict the offensive manoeuvres, which can be varied to suit individual fluctuations in the man-for-man. Outside shots over a screen can be used against a sagging defender, drives off a screen against a presser (page 122).

Eminent American coaches have filled large texts with hundreds of set plays to illuminate the seeker of basketball truth. Coaching journals are littered with the pet plays of all kinds of coach from junior grades upwards. I sometimes wonder if it is a worthwhile effort to write or read about these plays. With a knowledge of offensive fundamentals *it is easy to devise plays*—probably the easiest aspect of a coach's work. Moreover, only the team coach can know the precise demands and capabilities of his own players, and he has a unique combination of human beings who need a unique play if they are to be at their most effective. I may read 5,000 plays without finding one which suited my particular team. With far less effort, and much more self satisfaction, I could devise my own!

Situation Plays

Extremely formal set situation plays are much more common in the international scene that developed pattern plays. These are applied where many elements of a situation can be predicted quite accurately, where an exact pattern of player deployment and movement can be reproduced, and where an easily discernible signal can be given for the play to start.

Such situations mainly arise at

    a.   Jump Balls—especially where the likely winner of the tip can be predicted.

    b.   Free Throws—especially if on the shot where the ball comes into play its rebound direction can be predicted.

    c.   Out of Bounds.

Jump Ball. There are broadly three divisions of jump ball situations, losing, winning and indeterminate; and of course there are three positions for jump balls to occur—back, mid and front court. Depending upon the availability of practice time and the ability of his players, a coach will select *some* of these nine specific situations (3×3) as being the most productive, and design *scoring* plays for them. For example, winning jump ball situations in mid and front court should lead to a quick overload and attempted shot. For the other situations, a coach will have uppermost in his mind the problem of getting possession of the ball, or in really hopeless situations at least he can restrict the opposition to gaining possession in an unproductive area.

It has become conventional for all players to line up on or very near the circle at jump balls, even though they may break away from these starting positions during the initial phases of the play. We should define the 'offence' in jump balls as that team which is likely to win the tip. In that case, the defence will match the offensive pattern; and since the offence normally attempts to put all its players as close to the ball as possible, inevitably players end up neatly arranged around

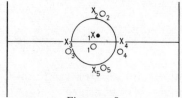

Figure 128

the circle (Fig. 128). It is important to remember that X_1 being likely to win the jump gives his team mates the advantage of selecting their positions, with the defence adjusting to

Plate 80 Typical line up at jump ball.

the safe side of the pattern. Since the jump ball is likely to be closely contested, even the winner is going to find that he has little space in which to develop force with the ball. He will be unable to do much more than a straight single arm tip (page 64), and the pass he makes cannot be expected to go much beyond the perimeter of the circle. If he does not have all his team mates on the perimeter, then the opposition could overload those who were within tipping range and interfere with their reception of the ball.

The offensive team have two problems: one, to ensure possession of the ball and two, to achieve a quick overload. The first of these is achieved by two players, the jumper and the receiver. Some arrangement is made to select a receiver— either a prearranged tactic, or a signal given by the jumper. The receiver should be a player who has a relative height advantage over his opponent. The pass can, of course, go in any direction, but most jumpers have a preferred tipping direction, which is usually anywhere in their frontal area (Fig. 129). The scope of a jumper's usefulness can be increased tremendously if he learns to tip with either hand. Then, he can select which way to face on the jump ball, which is valuable not only in terms of the direction of the pass, but also allows him to face the referee who is throwing the ball up—

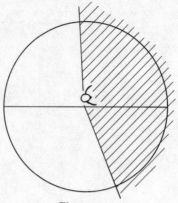

Figure 129

thus seeing the ball more clearly. In a mid or back court winning jump ball play the direction of the pass is not so critical since the ball has to cover a long distance to reach a shooting position. The extra few feet of a backwards tip may be well worthwhile if other factors in the play can be made more certain (Fig. 130 a). On the other hand, a front court play which tips away from the intended direction of the ball may waste precious time, and such plays tend to be more direct with the tip (b).

Plate 81 A winning jump ball play: lob forward and high from 14 to Williams who, though double teamed as the likely receiver, moves back to catch and pass immediately to 7.

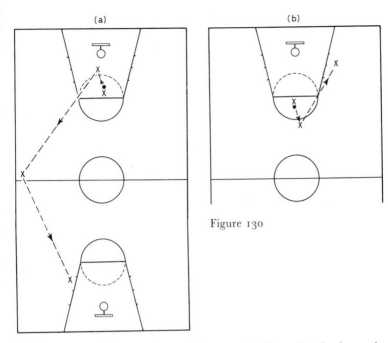

Figure 130

The second factor, the achievement of overload, depends upon that number of players which is necessary to outnumber the retreating defence. Initially, the offence can certainly release two players from the circle as the referee throws the ball, since it knows the ultimate direction of the tip, leaving one player as a 'safety man'. These breakaway players should try to deceive the opposition about their intentions. If the defence has played ultra-safe by keeping one player back, away from the circle, then the offence can afford to put an attacker alongside him, thus limiting and pressurising that defender. Figure 131 shows a typical set up with the tip going forward, and then a pass to the least likely man to be marked —having cut from the back, off a screen. He should be free, but is reinforced by the tipper *and* first receiver, with defensive balance being maintained by at least one team mate.

The second type of play is used at losing jump balls. Of course, when a team is certain that it will lose the jump it can merely retreat into a defensive formation, thereby conceding possession but avoiding immediate overload. The more

201

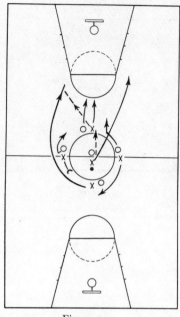

| Figure 131 | Figure 132 |

dynamic approach is to devise a method of intercepting the ball after it has been tipped. This involves predicting the likely direction of the tip (including faking a weak defence in that area), then suddenly overloading that area as the ball is tipped, simultaneously maintaining a defensive balance (Fig. 132). Such a play is successful if it merely gains possession, and most teams are content to achieve that aim on 30 per cent of the losing jump ball situations, not being particularly concerned with achieving a quick overload.

These have been a couple of examples of jump ball plays in specific situations. There are other situations, and an infinite number of other plays—but the principles remain the same.

Free Throw. Here there are four broad subdivisions of play, these being on offence and defence, with the shot being scored or not scored. Not many teams bother with set plays from a scored free throw, though there are obvious advantages for the defensive team to strike quickly, having gained possession from a scored free throw. The more common plays are designed

Plate 82 14 tips to 15; at the same time the least likely to break does in fact do so (7), and receives the next pass. He drives, followed by 14 and 15, with 8 and another maintaining defensive balance.

Plate 83 A losing jump ball play; Howgill (13) has refrained from jumping and is ready to cut; his four team mates have moved strongly into interception positions.

203

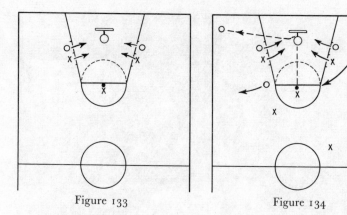

Figure 133   Figure 134

around the disputed possession arising from an unsuccessful
free throw. Within the local interpretations of the rule concerning entry into the key, the position and movements of at
least five players are very predictable (Fig. 133). In some
special cases even the direction in which the rebound will go
can be predicted by the offence, where a requirement for two
points rather than one will force the shooter to bounce the
ball to one side or other of the ring, but normally this direction
is not so predictable. However, the 'keyside' players should
enter the key under the assumption that the ball is rebounding
towards them, and time their entry and jump under that
assumption. In this situation, the defenders have a slight
positional advantage and, in a good play, an easier task to
perform if they merely have to tap the ball to a team mate
in a certain position rather than to catch it (Fig. 134). On the
other hand, the attackers have a more difficult task of starting
from an inferior position and getting enough relative height
to either catch the ball or take an immediate tip in shot. They
could, however, in a similar fashion to the defence, tap the ball
back to their own team mate standing on the free throw line.

Provided these tactics are pre-arranged, then within the less
predictable situation of a free throw rebound the chances of
capitalising on whatever opportunities come a team's way
can be maximised. However, the unpredictability of the
rebound toes mean that both teams should ensure defensive
balance which for the thrower's team generally means two
players lying back court, on the side of the overload—and also,

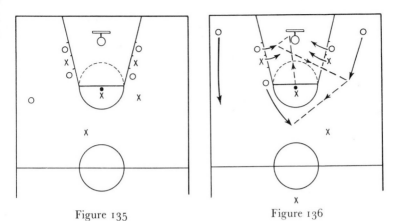

| Figure 135 | Figure 136 |

perhaps, the thrower immediately retreating into defence. For the defending team the line up usually leaves three or four players close to basket, outnumbering the offence, with one player acting as an outlet for the main pass. The relative height of the main defence rebounders decides how defensive minded the other defenders should be. If the defence has a decided advantage, then the three non-jumpers can look for a 3 v 2 (or 4 v 3) overload fast break (Fig. 136), each player starting his move as the free throw is taken. Faced with a situation like this, one would anticipate that the free thrower would immediately retreat, having released the ball, but usually he is too concerned about the fate of his shot and stands rooted to the free throw line!

Out of Bounds. This is the area where the majority of top class teams devote a great deal of time in perfecting a set play. Defensive techniques in this situation have been mentioned earlier (page 151), and the offence faces this problem with two main requirements. Firstly, they have to get the ball into play safely against a 4 v 5 situation on court. Secondly, they have to create a scoring opportunity. One can easily see the necessity for a special play to put the ball into court against an overload, but it is more difficult to understand why teams should add to this the problems of immediately freeing some-one for a shot, since the 4 v 5 situation makes even more difficult what is tough enough to achieve with 5 v 5! However, teams do it, and do it successfully against the odds, for the reason that the situation is a predictable one which allows the offence time to position itself exactly and **gives a precise signal for the start of the play**. This signal is usually the release of the ball by the referee to the thrower. The better plays then attempt to combine both requirements by freeing one or more players to receive a pass in such a position that they can take an immediate shot. The reader will have already gained the impression that I find the set out of bounds play somewhat illogical, but there is one time in the game when such plays are very necessary—when out of bounds with only a few seconds left for play in either half.

With the England team I have found the simple play shown in Figure 137 extremely successful, especially since it employs the basic principles of out of bounds plays very well.

Many out of bounds plays are more complex than this, especially in America where they have become something of a fetish! The American situation is also complicated by their local rule of having out of bounds balls from the base line (not allowed under international rules). A favourite method is to have a line up—a technique now copied extremely success-fully by association football players—near the shooting posi-tion (Fig. 138). Here, a simple beginning uses the line up as a multiple screen for X_1 to cut and shoot. As a complex switch is undertaken by the defence, then various attackers can cut through gaps into the space on the weak side, receiving either a pass direct from X_5, or one from X_1 on a 'pick and roll' basis. Other methods involve a line of four players with one or other of the centre players stepping out of line, the gap being closed by his team mates either side of him (Fig. 139). Un-fortunately, out of bounds plays which bring the receiver nearer to the passer generally allow the passer's defenders to sag and double team. Plays which take the receiver away from the passer make the pass a long dangerous one except in the U.S.A., where such a pass can be made from the *end* line to behind the free throw line.

Delayed Offence

It was mentioned earlier (pages 88 and 89) that time can be used as a weapon in both defence and offence. During the

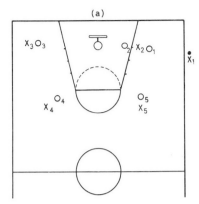

(a)

Fake. Basic set up, with X_2 acting
as most likely receiver of the pass,
being double teamed by O_1 and O_2.

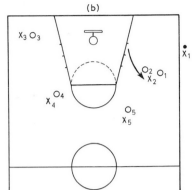

(b)

Divergence. X_2 creates a space
close to basket by cutting towards
the ball and faking to receive a
pass.

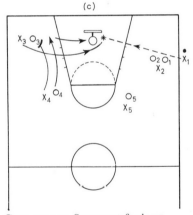

(c)

Convergence. Screen set for least
likely pass receiver X_3, who is our
very tall man (7 ft. 5 ins). As he
cuts the ball is passed to the near
side of the ring, where O_4 having
switched cannot reach the ball
because the ring and the net are in
the way. X_3 shoots.

Figure 137

 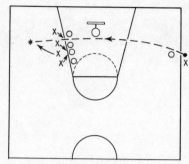

Figure 138   Figure 139

latter part of the game the losing team will normally attempt
to make better use of remaining time by increasing the pace
of the game and consuming less time in each offence. The
essentials of this type of play have been covered under fast
break (page 184), and pressing defence (page 147).

Conversely, the winning team have no such hurry, and one
can detect two distinct phases of closing play. The first is when
a team have such a lead that will probably win them the game,
but have not yet scored sufficient points to have a total which
is greater than the total their opponents might be able to
score. They therefore slow the play down, consuming as many
as possible of the thirty seconds they are allowed in which to
shoot. This depresses the overall score, and makes their lead
margin nearer the winning margin. For example, team A
leads by 80–68 with six minutes to go. At a normal turnover
rate of over two possessions per minute their opponents
would have at least twelve more possessions during the game,
with which if the tide turned they might score 20 points.
Therefore team B would finish with 88 points. During this
time team A *could* relapse, commit five violations, take seven
shots and miss four, eventually scoring 86 points. I have seen
this kind of thing happen to even the best of teams—eventually
losing from a winning position.

Now, if team A had taken about 26 seconds on each possession, with team B still maintaining their normal pace, there
would be three possessions per two minutes, giving nine
possessions each. Then (at the same rate) team B would score
15 points and team A at least 4 points. The final score would
be 84–83 to team A. So, without altering the 'turn of the tide',

which even the best of coaches can sometimes fail to do, the slowing down of play can save the game. This is called Stall offence—a vital weapon in any team's armoury.

The importance of stall is that the eventual aim must be to have a reasonable shot. Depending upon the make up of his team, a coach would probably consume about twenty seconds in merely maintaining possession (limited to an extent by the ten second rule for advancing the ball into the front court). The defensive possession tactics described on pages 22 and 61 are used here, a coach being fortunate if he has at least one specialist dribbler in his squad. Then the coach would give a signal for the offensive emphasis to change towards scoring, using whatever tactics he would normally employ against whatever defence faces him. Against the stall, defences will sometimes overcommit themselves, leaving an attacker completely clear for a high percentage close to basket shot. If this happens, then *irrespective* of the time, that player should receive the ball and shoot.

The converse is the case when a team enters the second phase of delayed offence. This occurs when team A have a sufficient score to be greater than the possible score of their opponents, even if team B score every shot and team A do not shoot at all but merely maintain each possession for thirty seconds. Here, *even a free player should not shoot,* since team A do not require more points—only possession. This is called a Freeze, and would be used in the situation where, with one minute ten seconds to go, team A have a 5 point lead. By retaining possession twice for the full thirty seconds, team A restrict their opponents to two possessions (and, incidentally, only ten seconds) in which time there is no opportunity to score 5 points.

During the last three minutes, teams using delayed offence *should not foul,* since this accelerates the rate at which their opponents can shoot. On the other hand the delayed offence, if fouled under 1970 regulations has the option of a new 30 seconds of possession from out of bounds at the half way line, or of taking two free throws. In general, during *stall* the option to have free throws should be selected, whereas during *freeze* the possession should be taken—this being merely an application of the differing aims of the forms of offence.

In both cases, the offence resolves itself into two phases. First, the ball is advanced into the front court, either to and in a shooting position or to avoid a ten second violation. This can be left to the star dribbler, left one on one if he is good enough, or helped by screens if necessary. If the dribbler is double teamed, then his free team mate should make himself available for a pass, and then get the ball back to the dribbler. Once in the front court the task becomes one of maintenance of possession, and also the development of a shooting opportunity in the case of the stall. This has implications for the ball handler, since he wishes during stall to keep the ball away from the shooting areas—the defence will tend to overload him, leaving space in the shooting areas into which the ball can eventually be passed. During freeze, the basket is unimportant since the offence do not intend to shoot. The only restrictions then are the half way line and court boundaries, *and* the three second area which should be avoided by *all* attackers like the plague. In general, convergence should not be used by the offence, since one dribbler ought to be able to maintain possession against one opponent. If double teamed, it is then relatively easy for him to pass to his free team mate, using the principles described on page 168. His team mates should not stand still, they should actively maintain divergence in order to give the dribbler room. They may even go via the back court to achieve a better position, since only the ball handler and ball have necessarily to stay in the front court.

Freeze play seems to arouse peculiar emotional states in Britain. It has always been a favourite method of mine, but it arouses hostile reactions from opponents and spectators of a most bitter form. Whilst everyone will applaud a teams efforts to win a game by denying their opponents the ball during rebounds, and by preventing their shooting when they do get the ball, they will be cruelly villified by denying their opponents the ball by freezing. To me this is as illogical as abusing a boxer for not allowing his opponent to hit him! The rules of basketball state that the aim of the game is to score *and* prevent one's opponents from scoring. The best legal way of achieving this is by denying them the ball, and the freeze does this *par excellence*!

Part 3 : Principles of control

Basketball is all about control. Even if one considers the wider educational, sociological, or even political effects of the game, the aim is to do something which achieves a certain effect. This is control.

If what we are concerned with is control, then the principles of control, which are well established, should be applied to the game in order to achieve the most effective control possible. It may be that the casual reader would wish to switch off here, wondering in fact what it has to do with basketball at all. That is his prerogative. The basketballer who really wishes to get the most out of the game, however, will find a whole new dimension of interest and involvement appearing before him if he can begin to see how intention and achievement, cause and effect, means and ends are linked in this, perhaps the most controllable team game in existence.

Control Theory

Control is achieved by the processing of information. This information can take many forms—it might be the words or gestures of the coach, the referee's whistle, the sight of the ball, the feel of the floor, a scouting report, a nerve impulse, etc., etc.

The original information is called the Input, which enters the control system and is put into code form for central analysis and processing. The end result of this evaluation of all the input information is a Decision to take a certain course of action. Messages to this effect are transmitted to the Effectors—the parts of the system responsible for making actions (in the human these are the muscles of the body). Here the information is decoded into movement, which is the final Output of the system. Let me show this now with some control diagrams. Figure 140 illustrates what most uninitiated basketballers deal with—a Black Box, in control terminology. All we know or care about is that information is presented to

Figure 140

the competitor, and he takes action with more or less success. By altering the input, we may cause a change in the output, and by remembering which inputs tend to give successful outputs we build up a store of successful control information which, in the experienced basketballer, may be wide enough to cope with the most of the situations he will face. This system is called Feed Forward Control, because all the information flows forward until the end result takes place.

All this is rather clumsy, though, and if we take the lid off our black box to discover how the inside works, we can see a much more complex system which, if carefully manipulated, can perform much more complex functions. In this system, each part of the output is monitored—allowing corrections to be made to the action while it is in progress. The control diagram (Fig. 141) illustrates an error checking device

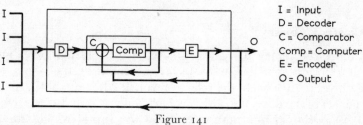

Figure 141

(Comparator) which compares the action messages, and the action itself, with a preconceived concept of what the action should be. If there is any difference between the intended and the actual action, the comparator changes the action messages in an attempt to achieve a better result. Since this system depends upon the feeding *back* of information, it is called Feedback Control.

All human activity is continuous from birth to death. There is never a stage during life when we can say 'I am now going to start taking in information, making decisions and taking actions'. There is already information within us stored up over

212

a period of years or seconds, so that we know what a ball is, how we are standing, how fast we are moving, where the basket is, etc., all of which can be called intrinsic information, as against the extrinsic information specifically concerned with *now* and coming from outside us. This is still Input, though it is already in coded form and stored in the central processor (computer). Another 'extra' about which we must be concerned is the effect of unforseen disturbances upon the system. The most perfectly executed jump shot is apt to go astray if the shooting elbow is jogged at the moment of release! Now our control diagram looks like this (Fig. 142).

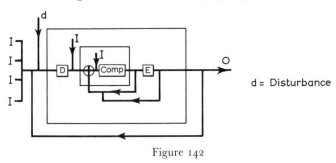

d = Disturbance

Figure 142

At this stage we should perhaps look at a couple of examples of control systems in basketball, illustrating both the broad principles and the interdependence of various units.

Firstly, let us take a player attempting to score. His total extrinsic input may be summarised:

1. Instructions called by the coach (fast break, draw the foul).
2. Information from team mates (go 1 on 1, we're backing up).
3. Opponent's position and movement.
4. Feel of the ball during the dribble.
5. Own position and pace (checking reference points, eg. sideline, walls, etc.).
6. Position of basket (late in the movement).

Added to this input, as he goes for the shot, is the disturbance of a violent push by his defender and a low bounce as the ball hits a dud floor board.

This information is received and coded by his sense organs—eyes, ears, touch, etc., and supplemented by his intrinsic input:

1. Coach's preliminary instructions.
2. Years of training and development.
3. Emotional state.
4. Knowledge of equipment playing characteristics (resilience of board and ring, grip of shoes, elasticity of ball, etc.).
5. State of own body (angles of joints, stretch in muscles, tiredness, etc.).
6. Team spirit, determination, fear of injury, etc.

A course of action is decided upon by the computer—a drive to the left of the defender into a height shot. Action messages are sent and the relevant muscles are activated. As the movement proceeds, information about it is fed back to the input, and compared with a mental image of what the movement should be. Small alterations are made to the action messages (eg. dribble lower, drop the right shoulder, move left away from contact). Then suddenly, the disturbance effects are felt and the computer realises that the first intention will not be successful. The range of alternative actions is reviewed, and a different one selected. Action messages are sent to reach down for the low bounce and to offensive roll to the right, finishing with a right hook shot. Feedback messages confirm the success of this manoeuvre, and additional input comes from a peripheral glimpse of second wave team mates coming for the rebound. As he takes off for the hook shot, the player sees that his opponent has stumbled, so he modifies his action messages again to reach up for a soft underhand lay in rather than a hook, since this has a higher probability of success.

Throughout this example, the reader will have noticed that actions are *modified* rather than changed. There is a very important reason for this. Action messages running along a nerve are rather like trains running along a track. *They cannot overtake one another.* So once an action message has been sent, it cannot be recalled. If a modifying message is sent soon enough, the action can be modified before it is too late. There is a fairly precise time scale laid upon this which depends upon the response time of the limbs concerned. Two approximate examples can be seen in the following chart:

Approx. time in tenths of seconds	Original action	Example 1	Example 2
0	Team mate free		
1	Information reaches brain	opponent moves	
2	Decision to pass ball	information reaches brain	opponent moves
3	Message goes to limbs	decision to stop pass	information reaches brain
4	Passing action begins	message goes to limbs	decision to stop pass
5	Ball released	release not made	message goes to limbs too late— ball has gone!

In example 1 the new information reaches the brain one tenth of a second after the original opening is perceived. The original action can be modified in time to prevent the ball being released. In example 2 the new information is two tenths of a second late, and the modifying message is too late to prevent the release of the ball. My own experiments have shown that once a decision to start an action has been taken (for instance, to begin a free throw) anything extra which happens after that point (even the lights being turned off) does not alter that part of the throw which takes less than 0.4 seconds. I suppose most players have experienced the helpless feeling of beginning an action involving the release of the ball, and being unable to stop the release even though knowing the ball is going to be intercepted or checked.

For my second application of control theory in basketball I shall use the example of the coach. His problem is a greater one in that he has to control the actions of other people, and to a great extent is limited by their control systems as well as his own. The total control diagram then becomes something like Figure 143.

In effect, his action messages have a double decoding system. First they are translated by his vocal cords and communicated to the players; second, they are decoded into actions by the players.

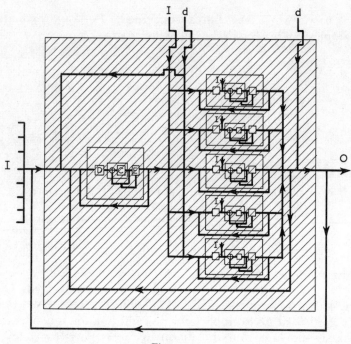

Figure 143

So, to illustrate this theory in practice, the coach is at the half time of a game. His extrinsic input consists of:

1. Opponents' tactics (from pre-game scouting and first half analysis).
2. Playing conditions (equipment, environment, spectators).
3. Refereeing standards.
4. State of the game (score, fouls, etc.).
5. Own player performance (first half analysis from statistics *and* players).

Most of this is in the form of information feedback from the game. His intrinsic input is his own stored knowledge of the game, his knowledge of his players' and the opponents' play and coaching characteristics, and his emotional and philosophical attitudes towards the game.

This information is then evaluated, and a decision made about the play in the second half of the game (say, to use a

216

weak side screen play). The decision is decoded, communicated to the players, and the game restarts. On the first two possessions four of the players have performed their function with little disturbance, getting a player free cutting towards basket. However, the input to the fifth player has not been efficient and he fails to make the pass to the cutter at the right time. Each time the pass is intercepted, and the feedback to the player *and* the coach is that the pass should be altered. The coach, who has the best mental image of the desired manoeuvre, receives a modification message from his comparator, which he transmits to the player concerned—telling him to make the pass a bounce pass and a little earlier. Next time, the player acts upon this clearer input, and the move is successful.

After a while, the opposition decide that the play is too successful, and change to a zone defence. This is a disturbance signal which is detected by the players and the coach as they begin their offence. The disturbance is of such magnitude that the play breaks down completely and a held ball is forced. The coach takes the opportunity to call a time out, and selects an alternative input (a 1–3–1 mobile offence) which he gives to the players. Realising that the desired output is a long range shot, he replaces two of the players with others who are more capable of that type of output. These go on court with an already acquired input concerning what they have seen and have had explained to them while sitting on the bench.

Here the coach has taken steps to avoid what is the biggest bugbear of basketball control—the decoding ability of the players. Just as a player's *muscles* have a certain degree of ability to decode the action messages sent by his brain, so do a coach's *players* have a certain degree of ability to decode the action messages sent by the coach's brain. And similarly, players tend to be particularly suitable for some action messages and not for others (both intellectually and physically). The coach has to ensure that the best possible combination of players is on court to carry out the specific action messages he sends. Different action messages may demand different players, and yet many coaches seem to be very reluctant to ensure this compatability of players and tasks.

During the first couple of offences against the zone, long

range shots are used which rim the ring and come out again. This error feedback is registered by the particular players and the coach, but this time the players' comparators assess the error and they compute a new flight path for the following shots which are much more successful. The coach receives this success feedback, and modifies an intention to give an error message to the players at the next opportunity.

At this stage I should mention two specialised principles of control which have great relevance in basketball. The first, which can be expressed by a formula well known to cyberneticians boils down to saying that disturbance effects are nullified when the action mechanism is very strong. Even the most delicate and skilful of player actions, or the most complex and sophisticated of team plays, will be less liable to disturbance errors if performed with a great reserve of strength. Teams such as the Russians and Jugoslavs have applied this principle *par excellence* in recent years, and have occasionally toppled the Americans from world dominance as a result. The principle applies at all levels however. For a given degree of skill, the stronger you are, the better.

Figure 144

The second principle concerns the overshoot effect of error controls. Figure 144 shows the type of oscillation which generally accompanies feedback control. Bicycle riding is an excellent example of this phenomenon, where correcting movements of the handlebars must always go slightly past the mid point and then swing back the other side. Riding a bicycle, even in a straight line, is virtually impossible if the handlebars will not move! Of course, if the oscillations go beyond a critical point of no return, then the error becomes irretrievable! Coaches must take care that error messages they give their players do not overshoot too far—they must expect a slight oscillation in their control of all aspects of their team's function, even in such control problems as discipline and morale!

Communication

I have made the point that control is achieved by processing information, and that information in its various forms has to be transmitted from one place to another—either within the body or between bodies. The transmission of information is called Communication, which in itself has become an extremely complex and sophisticated science. The principles of Communication Theory are basic to the work of the basketball coach.

As the concept of team games grew in the recreative environment of mankind, a desire for more efficient co-ordination between the individual units of any team saw the emergence of a controller who would decide upon the team's actions and communicate his decisions to the other players. Since no control could be achieved without communication, the most effective controllers were those who could best communicate, generally by virtue of their loud, penetrating and persistent voices. These attributes are still apparently the chief stock in trade of many of the controllers in modern sport!

The controllers, in their simplest form, were players called captains, but as the complexity of team control increased the captain evolved into the non-playing coach. In my opinion, the coach reaches his highest stage of evolution in the game of basketball, since this artificially invented and highly proscribed game gives greater and more constant power to the coach than any other game. The various stages in this evolutionary process were non-playing captains, managers, tactical advisers, etc., etc., the powers of each varying with the game and the governing bodies concerned. But, they all had to communicate.

Communication theory describes a transmitter as being the source of information, which is inevitably in the form of some code or other. The information is then sent via a communication channel or medium, and can be received by any receiver which is structured to accept the specific code being used, which lies within the communication medium and within range, and which is activated (switched on).

The three great problems of basketball communication are Noise, Error and Secrecy.

Noise

Here we use the word in its technical sense, that is any extraneous information which tends to obliterate the *communicated* information. This could be the actual noise of a large crowd of spectators, or could be the distractions of pretty girls in the front row, or the flashing of camera bulbs, or even the jumble of emotional and fatigue sensations in a player. Reception of the signal can be improved by the use of several techniques:

1. Signal volume can be amplified. The coach can shout, or wave his arms more violently. This can only work if *at the moment of transmission* the coach is capable of a greater amplitude of signal than the level of noise.

2. Signal frequency can be changed. Just as a radio set can be tuned and the transmission frequency selected to avoid noise from nearby wavelengths, so can a coach select a signal frequency which differs from the noise. For instance, a basketball crowd tends to give out a dull, low pitched roar. A high pitched signal even of fairly low volume can be heard above this noise (especially a shrill whistle), and coaches using a high pitched voice can be heard much easier by the players.

3. Signal range can be decreased—that is, the transmitter and receiver can be brought closer together. This has obvious implications during time out, when players and coach can get into a 'coaching huddle', but also during play when the coach cannot leave the bench, he should organise that at least one of the players (preferably the floor captain) passes close to the bench during transposition. This player can act as a relay, feeding the information to whomsoever is necessary, or all of, the team. This second stage of transmission is also in need of organisation, and can best be carried out at 'quiet' phases of the game— perhaps during stoppages, when all players should look to the captain for current information, or when a back court defence is waiting for a slow break to come up court.

4. Signal medium can be altered. If the 'noise' is audible then perhaps a visual medium could be used instead of an audible one. In this case, a 'call signal' is necessary so that the receiver will switch on. This call could be audible, or visual provided that the team have been trained to be constantly receptive to visual signals. For instance, a team can be trained to glance at the bench during *every* defensive transposition.

Error

No system is perfect. There will be error, and the form in which information is transmitted affects greatly the probability of error in both transmission and reception. The most common source of error in communication between humans is the code in which the information is transmitted—the language, in fact. How many flaming great rows have been caused by a failure to understand, rather than an actual difference of beliefs?

Even between basketballers, the technical language used is

Plate 84 George Wilkinson using vocal and manual communication with a Great Britain five. One might guess that there is some noise affecting the transmission!

liable to error. For instance, the word 'block' can be interpreted in several ways:

1. Contact with the ball made by a defender during an attempted shot.
2. An attacker positioning himself so that a team mate can shoot over him without being interfered with by a defender.
3. Physical contact by a defender on an opponent who does not have the ball.
4. A defender positioning himself to prevent an opponent taking a particular path.

Unless the word has been defined either specifically or by common usage between coach and players then there is a liability of error.

Not all of the technical code in basketball is composed of words: in many cases numbers are much more effective. We can see this especially in the numerical description of zone defences, and offensive positions. If the reader will attempt to translate '1–3–1 offence' into words he will see what I mean. The word versus numbers situation is dominated by the concept of Information Redundancy. This describes the extra length of any message over and above the absolute minimum necessary for that amount of information. Let us examine this concept in a concrete example. Assume that a coach wants his team to change from zone to man-for-man defence, his team being capable only of two defences. His instructions could be given in several ways, and their length measured in terms of the number of syllables used.

Message	*Length in Syllables*
Change from zone defence to man-for-man defence	11
Change to man-for-man defence	7
Play man-for-man	4
Change defence	3
Blue (this being a code name for man-to-man)	1

Obviously, the less redundant a message is, the more efficient it can be—but the more liable to error. For instance, if the coach was *very* excited and got mixed up in his transmission, the messages could come out like this:

1. Charge form snow defen to men to men defen
2. Charge to men to men defen
3. Pray men to men
4. Charge defen
5. Glue (this being a code word for freeze offence)!

In this situation, the more redundant the message, the less critical is the effect of error—though I hope that I never get quite that excited during a game! A player, hearing 1, 2 and 3 in a noisy situation, would probably still 'get the message' whereas 4 and 5 would be more confusing.

Another effect of redundancy is, of course, to increase the transmission time—or conversely to decrease the amount of information which can be communicated in any given period of time. Where time is very scarce, for instance during a brief lull in the game or during transposition, a highly efficient and less redundant code should be used. During longer stoppages, such as free throws or time outs, a happy medium can be struck between redundancy and length efficiency. When there is much time to spare, such as pre-game or half time briefings, redundancy comes into its own, especially since it allows also the development of the emotional undertones of a message.

The last consideration of redundancy introduces the concept of Repetition as an error combating mechanism. Especially with short coded messages, an immediate repetition of the signal (provided the transmission is correct) can reinforce the message to the receiver.

Secrecy

Of the total information a coach wishes to transmit to his team, some will be less effective if it is also received by the opposition whereas other information will be of no use at all to the other team. An example of the former can be seen in an instruction to set up a stealaway fast break. If the opposition realise that this shock tactic is being introduced, they will adapt their offence to improve the defensive balance. So, such an instruction must be given in secrecy—either by a low amplitude signal, or by a code which is not understood by the opposition.

On the other hand, personal advice to a player that his shots are unsuccessful because of a technique deficiency can be given without fear. 'Shoot a little higher' may work wonders for your player, and can hardly be of use to the opposition if they overhear it.

I hope that the reader has not been upset by this slightly scientific consideration of some of the problems of control. My own experience is that it makes the effects of different control methods easier to assess, and therefore permits a coach to select the most effective methods for his own personal use. Though I have considered information to travel mainly in one direction, it should be remembered that the control feedback described on page 212 includes communication from *player* to *coach*. The methods of achieving this are covered in greater detail on page 245. I shall now proceed to the more difficult and less objective considerations of the 'humanistic' problems of control, rather than the 'mechanistic'.

Success

Just how can we assess the success of a coach? It would be so easy to say that the more games a coach wins, the more successful he is. The best coach in the world would then be the coach of the world champions. If, however, this coach then took over the England team, he would not win the world championship, and yet he is still the same man, the same coach. Is he the best coach in the world? Perhaps not.

No team can do more than it is capable of doing, therefore a coach's success is limited by the capabilities of his players. In that case, the success of a coach is gauged by the amount of his team's *potential* ability that he can get them to produce on court. The best coach in the world is then the man whose team approaches nearest to its maximum potential. The control of play by the coach is always 'buffered' by the efficiency of his players (page 215), and his job then is not to devise weird and wonderful blueprints for victory, but to search for the key to unlock his players' store of ability.

This is still a very narrow view of successful coaching,

224

orientated around 'winning' or physical performance as the criterion of success. Though not really within the scope of this book, I must point out that the aims of sport are much broader than 'merely' winning, and that in situations where winning is not so important other criteria should be used to judge the success of a coach and his team. May I illustrate this point by looking at three of the teams I have coached, and how I assess my efforts with the teams.

In 1965 I took over the Welsh national team as player coach. Wales, with fewer than 1,000 registered basketball players, had been the laughing stock of British basketball for many years, and had never beaten either Scotland or England. My specified aim with the Welsh team was to win the International Championship, held annually between Ireland, England, Scotland and Wales. Dominated by this aim I concentrated my efforts on the seven best players and fanned their nationalistic fervour and individual confidence to such an extent that they went into the next championship really believing that they would win. Each player produced his best ever form during the tournament, which, combined with my destructive pre-game and game tactics, destroyed all opposition and won us the title. This was no flash in the pan, because in the next year we repeated the process, much to the delight of Welsh basketball and to the chagrin of our opponents.

When I first took over the England team, I was given the job of divorcing the squad from the standards of our domestic play, and putting them on a par with other European teams. This was to be a three or four year plan, and I selected about twenty young players to develop through this period. During the first couple of years I was to work on their techniques and team spirit, then to expose them regularly to better class opposition. Over the first twelve months, my aim was to develop team spirit, morale and absolute faith and loyalty to one another and to the coach. This we did, and for the first time ever, a national team became a closely knit family of basketballers, giving us all an emotional and morale development of the highest order. It is true, but incidental, that over this time we developed as human beings, both individually and collectively. At the end of the first year a serious car accident involving my family forced me to resign my position,

225

H

and the national team eventually fell apart even though individuals still went on to become very good players. It never reached the peaks that we had previously believed to be within our grasp.

My third example demonstrates a different aim again. Basketball in Britain has always existed as a players' game, played in an intimate atmosphere in small gymnasia, with fewer spectators than players and no publicity to speak of outside the game itself. My aim was to publicise and develop the game in one area, as an example to the rest of the country that basketball could be a big attraction in terms of spectator interest from non-basketballers, *and* that basketball could be financially self supporting. I managed to interest most of the top players in the area with the idea and we formed a team called Loughborough All Stars, staging 'Spectacular' promotions in the best spectator halls available. The game became linked with other events such as pop groups or other athletic demonstrations at half time, preliminary games of local interest, dances after games, a restaurant and a bar. Piped music, cheer girls and running commentaries helped to develop the atmosphere. Programme sellers, autograph hunters and attractive posters added to the picture. Most of all, the game had to be attractive, with colourful uniforms, exciting individual performances, extrovert showmanship, sympathetic refereeing and above all—*close finishes* (deliberately engineered by judicious selection of opponents and use of substitutes). I had one season with the club before transferring my job to another area. In this time we played a dozen home 'spectaculars', developing a large and enthusiastic following from within a radius of twenty miles, reaching the semi-finals of the national championships, and ending the season without each player having had to reach deep into his pocket to play the game.

Now, in each of these cases, the coaching aims had been completely different, and yet there had been a great degree of success. Looked at with other criteria in mind, each could have been assessed at almost complete failure: The Welsh team had failed to raise the overall standards of basketball and had destroyed the confidence and integrity of other national teams; the young English team had failed to reach its eventual

Plate 85 a, b and c Winning: Wales take the International Championship. Social: Loughborough celebrate a good season. Spirit: Togetherness after a tough game.

aims in European basketball; the All Stars took players from other local teams, causing antagonism and break up in other clubs than itself. To me, my greatest success as a basketballer coach was with my first England squad, though the England squad I have at present will probably be even more successful eventually. These are situations where I think and act as an 'educator' in the broadest sense of the word; where the value of the individual is paramount; where the national team is an expression of the ideals and mores of the nation. To me 'why and how you play' is much more important than 'who you beat'.

However, as an author I have also a duty to help the reader in his search for methods of achieving success in other aims— particularly of winning games. So my following comments are based upon the assumption that *winning* is the major aim. It is up to each reader to modify these principles to suit his own particular criteria of success.

227

Player Control

Each player has a function to perform on court, a desired output which is a product of his own and the coach's intentions. The control of his own movement is achieved by his nervous system which can operate at many different levels. Virtually every action he makes is in response to a stimulus of some description or other; the referee tosses the ball, the player jumps; an opening occurs, the player shoots; a team mate signals, the player passes—and so on.

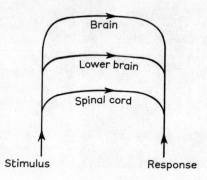

Figure 145

There tends to be a sliding scale of nervous involvement in this stimulus—response phenomenon (Fig. 145). At the one end lie the purely reflex actions where the computer analysis of information (page 212) is by-passed. These are the fastest responses, and can be inborn (such as the eye blink when a ball approaches the eye) or learned (such as the withdrawal of the ball when an opponent attempts to snatch it away). These actions actually start *before* the brain becomes conscious of the situation, though afterwards the movement *may* reach the level of consciousness. The eye blink reflex, for instance, might occur without the player being conscious of it at all.

The medium response involves a higher level of the nervous system, where a fairly complex co-ordination may be necessary. For example, a driving player who is forced to swerve suddenly by a player appearing in his path will perform most of the necessary movements automatically. Some of what he does will be appreciated and analysed consciously, but the majority of the action will be dealt with in the lower brain, and because of this, the response to the stimulus is still quicker, though not as quick as the pure reflex.

The conscious response may be to either a very complex stimulus, or a very unusual one, so that the player cannot really begin the movement proper until he has analysed the information and consciously decided what to do. This can be seen in a pick and roll play (page 126) where the ball handler has to wait until he sees the movements of the defenders before knowing whether or not he should pass to his team mate.

The player, in learning to control his movements, has to decide (or have decided for him) which elements of his play need to be 'uncomputed' reactions or reflexes, and which need to be analysed as responses to varying situations. The first type can be called 'Conditioned Responses', and are trained and developed in a very specific way. The second type I shall call 'Analytic Responses', which demand a very different form of development.

Conditioned Response

The game of basketball has many elements which are almost identical each time they occur. One thinks immediately of the free throw as a total action which is virtually identical each time (or should be). But even within total actions, there are parts of actions which are virtually identical—the grip on the ball, stance at a jump ball, body position, defensive position, etc. Permutate these parts and we finish up with a whole variety of different complete actions with which to cater for the variety of situations comprising the game. Obviously, these identical elements should be learned in such a way that the player can perform them without thinking about them, thus allowing him to concentrate on other elements of the total action which need analysis.

The conditioning of responses can be achieved in a quite straightforward way. The required stimulus is presented to a player, for example a ball being passed to him at chest height. He is told how to catch the ball—perhaps even shown how to do it. When he achieves a successful catch he is rewarded, perhaps by feelings of success or by praise from the coach. The process is repeated time and time again, success being rewarded, and failure being punished by scorn or a tongue lashing! Eventually the movement becomes 'grooved' into the player, so that the presentation of the stimulus is followed automatically by the catch. From this stage on, the coach should gradually reduce the input given to the player so that he needs to devote a decreasing amount of his attention to the actual catch, and can concentrate on something else. This part of the training can be achieved by allowing the player a first glimpse of the approaching ball later and later in the flight, and then by getting him to look away from the ball earlier and earlier in the flight. Eventually the player will become so highly skilled that he can see a ball coming quite late in its flight, automatically adjust his arm position, and then look away at the rest of the play leaving his body to complete the catch automatically.

Very great care should be exercised by basketballers in selecting the 'grooved pathways' which they will develop. Once such an action has been started, it will tend to continue *even if it becomes obvious that it will fail!* Let us take an example of a coach who believed that a jump shot should be taught in this manner. He taught his player that every time he received the ball in shooting distance to bend his knees, carrying the ball in two hands above the head, then to jump high extending legs and arms, finally releasing the ball at the top of his jump with the right hand pushing, left hand supporting. He grooved the pathways, and the player became extremely accurate with this shot. The player played for several seasons in minor leagues, achieving great success, which reinforced his jump shooting technique. Then the team were promoted to a tougher league, and our jump shooter found that when he clicked into his set response to the stimulus of a jump shooting opportunity, there was an opponent in the air above him batting the ball out of his hands, or another man jogging his shooting elbow, or less time for the jump. His success rate dropped, and yet he knew no other way to perform a jumping shot. He had been prevented by his stereotyped technique from achieving the ultimate potential of which he was capable.

Analytic Response

As a broad view, this theory treats the game of basketball as a whole. The player starts his movement from the first whistle (or even before), *modifying* that movement by the inclusion of identical elements and of unique movements and permutations, in response to the changing stimuli as the game progresses. *He functions then in response to the feedback of his own involvement with the game, and can never be certain what his next move will be, since it will be modified at all points by the effect it has on the total situation.* There will, of course, be a tendency for some actions to be followed by others—even a plan that they should. Loss of possession will tend to be followed by a retreat to defence, first wave fast break by a second wave, shots by rebounds, etc. This involves the predictions of events, but no prediction can be 100 per cent, in fact many are as low as 50 per cent! The modification of response takes care of the unpredictable part of the game, turning automatons into geniuses!

Now, if we are to leave the analysis of the changing situation to the player, it is too much to hope that he will be naturally equipped to deal with the tremendous complexities at which we have only begun to hint on page 213. He is presented with a 'Display' of information which includes everything his senses are *capable* of picking up (whether they do or not). The human receiver does not have the capacity to appreciate *everything* in the display simultaneously, nor does he need to. After all, there are only a few items in the display which critically affect his own performance—these are the ones he should be trained to detect, the remainder should be ignored. Figure 146 shows the kind of selection he might make, considering only the *extrinsic* information—not the *intrinsic* (page 213).

Having learned to discriminate the relevant information from the display, the player must then process it. Even though he has reduced the total amount of information, it is still a large task to perform the analysis, and he will do it more efficiently if he has 'programmes' in his computer. *These programmes are the principles of play which formed the first part of this book,* and for highly developed players will include many group

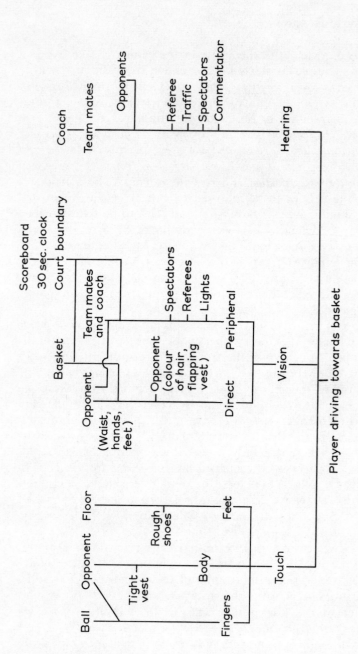

Figure 146

tactical considerations as well as the individual fundamentals.

In the majority of basketball training, therefore, the coach should expose the players to wide varieties of situations, teaching them to modify their movements, and permutate their identical elements, according to basic principles of play. This is not easy coaching, for player or coach, but it is the most rewarding in terms of personal satisfaction and eventual development. It puts a premium on the player who blends intelligence with physical ability—the educated sportsman, in fact. Our conditioned response jump shooter (page 230) would in these circumstances merely have applied his relative height programme (page 44) to have continued his successful career!

Coach Control

Each of the five players performing on court controls his output using the total input described earlier, which includes the basic instructions and the continuous advice communicated to him by the coach. It would be too much to expect that everything the *player* thinks he ought to do on court should tally with what the *coach* thinks the player ought to do. The situations where there is a difference of opinion provide a source of conflict which cannot only destroy the efficiency of coach control, but also prevent the player from achieving his own optimum control of output. Unfortunately, the more intelligent the player becomes, the more likely it is that he will develop his own views of what constitutes the 'right thing to do'—and these may clash with the plans of the coach. Yet, the coach wants to develop the intelligence of his players, and the more successful he is in this respect the more difficult he makes his own task of controlling them. Where the coach has in fact been responsible for the development of the 'physical wisdom' of his players, it is more likely that the players' opinions can lie closer to the coach's. This situation arises unfortunately rarely, except in cases where the coach's development and progress accompanies that of his players. Examples such as Ken Charles and Tony Smith spring to mind from the English scene—both being very successful schoolteachers coaching their pupils. As the players

H*

Plate 86 England Team 1962, with assistant coaches Ken Charles and Tony Smith. A half of the team were products of the coaching environment of these two men.

developed beyond school, their contact with the coaches was maintained at club level, through representative basketball finally to international level. The wheel finally turned full circle when the players themselves became coaches, one in fact returning as teacher and coach to the original school.

This type of situation allows for a parallel development of coach and players, a uniformity of thought, and a buffer against conflict. The one major drawback is that the faith the players have in the coach tends to be a specific one to that situation, and associated with one generation of players. As new players come through into the representative scene, who have not been developed along the same lines as the coach, the resultant conflict destroys the efficiency of the control system, and it becomes extremely difficult for that coach (however talented and well intentioned) to maintain his previous effectiveness.

The more common system is for players to progress from one environment to another in their climb to the top of the tree—school, minor club, major club, local representative, area representative, international—and of course for coaches to make similar progress. At the peak of development, players and coaches tend to be operating in several teams during a season, drawn from the top four categories mentioned. Coaches and players have therefore to adapt themselves to each situation, and devise methods of negating the conflict problems *which are bound to arise.* May I quote the example of the first team I ever coached. It was the England Men's team, which met as a group for the first time at the station departing for the European Championship tournament in 1962, beginning two days later. For many of the group, including me, we were complete strangers—never even having seen one another play! Needless to say, we didn't win any games, but we all learned a great deal about conflict resolution! Within a few days we in fact developed a very good working relationship, and eventually put up some surprisingly good performances against outstanding opposition.

As another example, this time of the opposite effect, consider the 1968 British Olympic Squad, in which I had the honour to play. The squad had about a year's preparation together, *and yet the best performance from the squad was its very first game.* From that point on there was a steady deterioration which was not even solved by desperately drafting in several new players just before the Olympic competition. The whole squad was riddled with conflict problems which could not be resolved.

The examples I have used have been taken from top levels of basketball, but the principles apply at all levels. We are commonly faced with the problem of blending the efforts of players and coaches of different origins and development, with different ideals and motivations, and with different methods of play. Little wonder that teams so often fail to realise their full potential. How can these sources of conflict be avoided or negated?

Respect. This is the first principle of efficient team control. The players must respect the motives, method and ability mainly of the coach, but also of their team mates. The central unit of this respect, though, is the coach. He is the focal input of the team. There must be no inherent noise in his communication with the team.

There are obviously many, many ways of achieving respect, but they fall mainly into three broad divisions:

1. Social
2. Emotional
3. Technical

Some social environments favour the coach in his relationships with the players. This can occur through tradition, as in the U.S.A., where a long history of coach dominated sport has led to a tendency of automatic acceptance of the coach's methods. That American coaches are well worthy of respect is beyond doubt, but much of that respect comes from an inbuilt feeling of the American player that he *should* respect the coach. For this reason, the American player is very easy to coach—not only does he have great talent, but a willingness to follow the coach's instructions. I can well remember the look of complete surprise on the face of Bill Bradley (acclaimed the world's finest amateur player) during half time of a British Universities representative game. This great American, having come to Oxford for a year, was playing for us in an international match, but even so we had not played too well in the first half. During the half time briefing the coach (a very eminent and respected man in British basketball) asked Bill his opinion about our playing methods for the second half. Even Bradley, the world's greatest, would not expect to be consulted so openly during a time when the coach is attempting to gain an effective control of his team's play!

In some other social environments there is an automatic respect for authority of any description, for instance in most basically socialist countries. Here again, the coach will find it easier to rely on the respect of his players and to obtain efficient control. School and other institutional situations provide similar conditions, though to a lesser degree. In the 1960 Olympic competition I was fascinated to see the coach of one Southern European team get up from the bench, go to one of his seated substitutes, and slap him hard across the face for some reason or other which I never discovered! The player just sat there and took it—I would have got up and floored the coach, and I imagine so would the majority of other players in Britain! The British social environment is different (and so are many other countries). There, without tradition and social structure to help him, the coach has to achieve respect in other ways.

The second method is emotional. Players will 'do or die' for a coach whom they regard with an affection close to love, or who acts as a focal point for a nationalistic, regional, or institutional fervour. Without wishing to go too deeply into the psychological aspects of human performance, I feel that it is such an important part of team control that we should consider it briefly.

The human is aware of all things through his 'psyche', his appreciation of everything around and within him is psychological. In all aspects of his performance there are limits or barriers, some of which are relatively unalterable (such as reach height), but most of which are arbitrary (such as intelligence, skill, power). These latter limits, appreciated psychologically, are called 'Psychological Barriers', but in the main they are artificial and depend only upon each individual's belief as to what he is capable of, or can tolerate. Through training, each player becomes competent at the fundamental aspects of the game. He can move, jump, throw, and catch, and occasionally does these with such great success, such a high level of skill, that he gets a glimpse of what he could really be like if only he could maintain that 'flash in the pan' performance. I am not talking about the occasional lucky shot which defies all the rules, but those occasions which most people infrequently experience when they see so clearly, feel so strong, think so quickly that they *know* they are going to succeed. This can all be summed up in one word, 'confidence' —confidence about one's skill, confidence in one's ability to tolerate painful feelings of fatigue, confidence in one's ability to overcome physical resistances.

With such confidence, the artificial barriers to player performance are pushed nearer to the real barriers, the actual capacity of which the player is really capable. In some of these areas, such as organic function, control mechanisms in the body take over and limit the function before the human reaches a level of performance which endangers himself. The healthy basketballer cannot push himself to such a stage of exhaustion that he drops dead, though when highly motivated he *can* contract muscles so forcibly that the tendon snaps or a bone splits. These control barriers cannot be overcome without the use of artificial stimulants, mainly drugs but also probably hypnosis. As far as the basketball coach is concerned, his job is to train the capacity and increase the confidence of his players so that the psychological barrier is pushed as near to the control barrier as possible.

The emotional stimuli a coach will use to achieve this psychological state will vary enormously, depending upon the personality of the coach and his players, and the social environment in which they play. Fear, anger, love, enjoyment, hate—all may have a part to play, and should be carefully selected and manipulated by the coach. I am ashamed to relate the story told to me of one American coach who, in his pre-game briefing of an English representative team against a Czechoslovakian squad, finished up a dogmatic tirade against his opponents with some such comment as '. . . now we're going to go and lick these Commie bastards'. I watched the game, and must admit that the defensive play that I saw from the English players on that occasion was the finest I had ever seen. They *were* motivated—I just don't happen to condone that particular method—the ends did not justify the means in my opinion. My shame was not for the coach, whose philosophy of the game was different from mine, but for the players who proved capable of being motivated in this way. Hate for one's opponent is undeniably a successful motivational tactic, but one which many sportsmen believe to be an inhuman one, which lessens the dignity and value of sport and sportsmen.

Such negative approaches to a game have essentially and eventually a self destructive effect. If one belittles one's opponents, then one's own performance against them is belittled. For instance, if I say that our opponents are a poor team, and beat them by two points, then we are by my own estimate also poor. If I say that they are a great team, but that we are greater, and then win by two points, even if our

238

play had been of exactly the same standard on each occasion we are by my own estimate a great team.

A coach must beware of the emotions he arouses in his team, being careful that at all times he maintains complete honesty and integrity with his players. Respect is not possible without trust—the player must be able to believe what the coach says. A coach may temporally achieve success by deceit, but repetition of that success will not be likely if the players discover that deceit.

The third aspect of a coach's capacity for inspiring respect from the players is his technical ability. This again falls into two categories, practical and theoretical. On the practical side, a coach can better deal with a player's development and performance if he has his own experience as a player to call upon. Not only can he demonstrate what he wants, but he knows the *feeling* of a movement or a manoeuvre, which helps him to transmit that to the player. But, even more important, a player will respect what the coach tells him when he knows that the coach has himself been an outstanding player using these methods. During the early part of my international coaching career, I was a better player than my players were. When I taught them the methods they should use, the respect they had for my ability helped them to acquire these methods. Now that age has played its familiar part, I am no longer better than my players, and it is more difficult to get them to accept that my methods are worthy of adoption. I hope that my reputation is sufficient to maintain a necessary level of respect—but on the occasions that I feel a certain diminishing of that respect I allow myself the luxury of reminding my players (in some subtle way!) of my past exploits!

For these reasons, a coach must be wary of scrimmaging *with* his team. His methods of play should be impeccable, maintained by practical training if necessary. Any inability he has by comparison with his players *must be seen to be* a consequence of advancing years and lack of training, rather than a basic inferiority of playing standard.

The aspect of technical skill is, of course, the coach's theoretical and tactical ability. Here the player must be in no doubt that the coach is at least better qualified than the players, if possible better than any other available coach, and

—most beneficial of all—better than any other coach in the country (or world)! The point is, how can the players become convinced of this?

We are involved here with an assessment of coaching ability, and the players will have both their own assessment, and the assessment of others whose opinion they value, to form their eventual conclusions. In general, the first opinion the player forms is one based upon other people's assessments. This forms the coach's reputation, which comprises his grade awarded by examination, his status by appointment (eg. the national team coach is the best available coach in the country), and his reputation by hearsay (including coaching record and grapevine fables).

Eventually, after having worked together for some time, the player will amend this first impression because of his own experience with the coach. This will grow as a product of games won and lost, player development, morale, enjoyment, etc., etc. This final assessment is the one which becomes the bedrock of each player's, and the team's, development. The team cannot really begin to make real progress until it reaches this final assessment, and then only if its assessment is a favourable one leading to the development of the necessary respect.

Confidence. In this, the second of our factors dealing with conflict in team control, we expand somewhat on the motivational confidence already mentioned in the previous section (page 238). That dealt with the confidence a player has in his own ability, but quite obviously each player need also to be confident of his team mates' ability otherwise he will play with reservation and a lack of commitment to the team effort. If all players are self confident they will play well and therefore tend to earn their team mates' confidence at the same time. A coach can enhance this effect by ensuring that each player's contribution to the game lies within the specific abilities of that player. A player then has the awareness that the team plan provides him with team mates who are capable and confident of performing specific play aspects, *and can rely upon them to fulfil their function.* Conversely, each player's function must be seen to be of significance, even if it may involve him in spending little time on court during games. For instance, the star centre in a team can only play at full pace for limited periods, needing three or four short rests of a couple of minutes during the game. His substitute knows that his function is to provide this short relief for the star, and that if he does not perform his function well the coach could not afford to take the star off. This would result in the star playing at less than full stretch, with a consequent lowering of team efficiency. Even though the playing standard of the two players differs, *together they are a one hundred per cent centre for a full game.* There is little point in saying that either is the more important, they are both completely necessary, and can build up a joint confidence based upon these principles. Expand these to cover all twelve players and you have a team in the fullest sense of the word. Conflict between players is reduced.

Our next consideration of player confidence is bound up with security of position. Virtually all players want to play, on court, for a reasonable part of the game. Some achieve this by playing with teams having a low enough general standard to ensure they get a full game. Others try to achieve it by developing their own abilities to a level which earns them a place on court in increasingly talented teams. This is the ambitious player, the one who poses us the more difficult problems. By his very ambition, he is really saying, 'I want to improve my play so as to become worthy of being a member of a higher standard team'. The 'highest standard' team might be his school or club first team, his district or area team, the national squad, or if already in the national squad, the team, or even the first 'five'. Now, part of this ambition is merely to achieve the status attached to team membership, but in the main the ambition is to achieve a 'grading' of his ability, this 'grade' being the actual playing standard of the team concerned. It is not enough 'merely' to be an international, the national team standard must also be recognised of 'international' level.

The importance of this principle is that for the player on the way up the ladder, he sees his way into a 'team' blocked by another player. If the established player was not so good, or became off form, the developing player could achieve his desired promotion. But, the standard of the team *is* the standard of that established player, so that promotion by a destruction or decay of an established player's ability is achieved at the cost of *lowering* that very standard which the ambitious player is trying to achieve. This would be anomalous, a negative of development. Far more worthwhile, and satisfactory, is for the ambitious player to *overhaul* the established one, thus incidentally raising the achieved standard. It is vital that coaches develop this *positive* approach from their ambitious players, the *negative* approach destroys standards.

The conflict arising from this situation then becomes a purely personal one, within the player, and can act as a motivational drive in his own development. The wise coach will be alert for signs of the conflict becoming open, *between* one player and another, beause while it *might* motivate one or other to develop, it will almost certainly destroy something which is even more important—team cohesion.

Conversely, the established player should have a confidence in his own performance by virtue of his membership of a high standard team, or first 'five'. In this case, he should realise that the minimum standard for membership of the team is set by the level of ability of the ambitious player. The established player knows that to belong to the team he merely needs to be better than those outside the team. The higher the standard of the ambitious, the higher is the 'necessary' standard of the established. It is a continuing compliment to him if his 'inferiors' are very good. So he has a vested interest, and motivation, in seeing their standards develop along with his.

On these principles, it is possible to develop an extremely positive attitude in a squad, competitive and yet sympathetic. Each established player must be made to feel a certain amount of security in his position. He must not think, as he goes up for a shot, '. . . if I miss this my position is in jeopardy', but rather, '. . . I have my position *because* of my ability, therefore I shall probably score'! The coach must openly demonstrate his faith in his players. If he considers them worthy of being on court, then he must back up that decision by giving them a fair opportunity to demonstrate that he is correct in his assessment. Of course, all players have off days, or off moments, but the long term approach must be of a two way faith between coach and players, leading to a confidence born of mutual co-operation and security.

Administration. Basketball is not just a matter of ten players and a ball. Everything surrounding the game requires a process of administration. The rules, the score, the facilities, the equipment, food, finance, travel, leagues, tourneys, injuries, health, etc., etc., all need to be well administered if destructive conflict is again to be avoided. Methods of administration really lie outside the scope of this text, but the club or organisation should be concerned about its attitudes and underlying principles of administration.

Firstly, there is a process of administration which is imposed upon the team by the governing body of the sport. Referees, table officials, rules, leagues, etc., are all defined and proscribed by 'them', being a nebulous term of abuse which most sportsmen feel towards officialdom! However, 'us' have to put up with 'them' if the game is to be played at all successfully, and a team should develop a good humoured acceptance of all these external administrations, whilst reserving the right to make proper representations to the administrators over points of difference. This builds up a fund of goodwill, within which any margin of error and difference will tend to go towards those sharing in the goodwill.

Nowhere is this more evident than with those most intimate of administrators, the referees. These people, devoted to the avoidance or prevention of conflict during the game, seem very often to be the major *causes* of dispute. However, one must accept that the great majority of referees do not want conflict and dispute in their game, in which case, those players or teams who co-operate with officials in these pacifying efforts must eventually earn the respect (and perhaps the bias in doubt?) of these officials. My early career was punctuated at frequent intervals by pitched battles with referees, only in cases where the referee was very weak did I ever come off a winner over officialdom. Though I might win an occasional point by browbeating the ref., in the long term they became biassed against me. As my reputation as a referee baiter grew, I found myself generally with seven opponents on court, with referees vying with one another to catch me out on all sorts of little tricks, both real and imaginary. It became a kind of game within a game, and my persecution complex grew at an alarming rate.

Eventually, mainly through the good sense and advice of my wife, I saw that everybody was a loser in this situation—except my opponents. So I changed completely, restraining myself to the best of my ability from verbally assaulting referees, and forbidding the slightest expression of hostility from my players (on pain of being benched). The effect was amazing. Referees with whom I had maintained a lifelong vendetta now became fans. I could truthfully say, at last, I did not mind who refereed my games.

To a lesser extent, the same attitudes must be developed towards other elements of external administration. A team has to accept the hierarchy, so 'if you can't beat 'em—join 'em'!

On the other hand, the internal administration of a team can be viewed in an entirely different light. It is not enough to devise administrative methods which are merely expedient. The whole nature of a team can be affected by the methods used to run that team, so these methods must reflect the nature (or the desired nature) of the team. To take a simple example, a coach may wish his players to feel that their basketball ability makes them important, that they are some kind of 'superior beings'. Even though in an amateur squad it might be more expedient for the players to wash their own uniforms, having them laundered professionally and waiting on hangers in the dressing room would possibly prove to be a worthwhile investment in terms of developing confidence.

In the majority of cases, it is better for the internal administration of a team to be the responsibility of a non-player. It is surprisingly easy to find non-players who eagerly welcome the opportunity of belonging to a team, especially when their function within the team is seen to be of great importance. Having a team manager relieves the coach and the players of the problems of administration, particularly immediately prior to, and after, the game. They can then concentrate their attention on the game itself. The team manager, with the advice and co-operation of the coach, should really plan his contribution to the team effort most carefully, analysing the effect each part of his function has. To me, a good team manager is more important than any single player, and a coach and manager who have the patience and intelligence to develop a good working relationship can work wonders for any team.

As mentioned earlier (page 224) one of the important aspects of team control is the information feedback from players to coach. A certain amount of this is of course achieved during the game, but a more formal organisation is often necessary, where players can put their points of view and suggestions about play, where democratic decisions concerning the running of the team can be taken, and where administrative details for future occasions can be worked out. An extension of this function can be achieved by using the captain as the representative of the players, especially in acting as their spokesman on matters which may be too delicate for general discussion. During the early part of a team's existence, the captain might find this to comprise a large part of his function, but if the team develops positive and sympathetic attitudes, the occasions for private discussion of major details between coach and captain will decrease.

Before leaving the topic of administration I should like to consider two rather special features, player coaching and assistant coaching. It will often happen that the only or best person to coach a team is one who still plays the game at a sufficient standard to warrant inclusion in that team as a player. Of course, the circumstances surrounding each individual case will differ, and one should be wary of making hard and fast general judgements. However, a team needs both a coach and players, and if one person has talents to offer in both departments then there are difficult decisions to be made. If I attempt to analyse the possibilities subjectively, I will need several thousand imprecise words—so I shall instead resort to hypothetical numbers to illustrate my points.

Imagine that the total possible effect of a team in one game is measured as 500 units by the players, and 100 units by the coach. This assesses the value of a good coach as about equal to having a sixth player on court! If there are (say) 10 players used, first five players being worth 70 units and second five 30 units, then each player and his substitute comprise 100 units of effectiveness. With a non-playing coach of 100 units, total effectiveness is 600 units. If the coach plays, and is worth 70 units, he replaces a 30 unit substitute—giving 540 units of playing strength. If his replacement as coach is at least a 61 unit coach, then the total team effectiveness will be increased. If his replacement is at most a 59 unit coach, then effectiveness is reduced. If by playing, the coach reduces his playing efficiency to 60 units, and his coaching efficiency to 90 units, total team effectiveness is even greater. If his playing efficiency drops to 40 units, and his coaching efficiency to 70 units, total team effectiveness is greatly reduced. If player coaching affects neither his playing nor coaching efficiency, total team effectiveness is maximum. All these are illustrated in Figure 147.

	Player Units	Coaching Units	Total
Non-player coach	$(5 \times 70) + (5 \times 30)$	100	600
Non-player coach	$(6 \times 70) + (4 \times 30)$	70	610
Non-player coach	$(6 \times 70) + (4 \times 30)$	50	590
Player coach	$(5 \times 70) + (1 \times 60) + (4 \times 30)$	90	620
Player coach	$(5 \times 70) + (1 \times 40) + (4 \times 30)$	70	580
Player coach	$(6 \times 70) + (4 \times 30)$	100	660

Figure 147

It should be obvious from this rather hypothetical example that anything is possible on the player-coaching scene. We cannot measure the various elements as precisely as I have pretended, but we can attempt to gauge the effects of various permutations of team and coaching units. The scheme does not include one very important possibility, that coaching effectiveness is maximum. All these are illustrated in Figure 147. on this point, consideration needs to be given to coaching function *during the game*, the different elements of which can be summarised thus:

    a.   Tactical analyses and decision making.
    b.   Communication with playing five.
    c.   Balance of playing and substitution strength.
    d.   Preparation of and making substitutions.
    e.   Communication with table.

Of these five, c, d and e, can all be done better by a bench coach. Point b, can be better done by a player coach. Point a is *usually* done better by a bench coach, but can *in some individual cases* be better performed by a player coach. Since a and b are probably the two most important functions, there is obviously a good case to be made for the advantages of player coaching *provided that the individual concerned is able to combine the functions efficiently*. I must say that at first class level, such individuals would be very rare indeed, but at lower levels they would become much more common.

Even for a bench coach, functions a and b are extremely demanding, and if he concentrates most of his attention upon them he tends to neglect the other three to a certain extent. However, these three less demanding tasks are such as can reliably be performed by someone assisting the coach. The basic instructions are given by the coach, acting upon information including that which the assistant has given him. The assistant coach then relays this information to the substitutes, and effects the necessary changes. For example, the assistant constantly surveys the playing five for signs of fatigue or malfunction, and keeps check on the fouls committed, points scored, rebounds taken, etc. This information he passes to the coach either upon demand, or when it becomes necessary. The coach decides what changes should be made, and if any substitution is necessary he tells the assistant which players to put into the game, and any brief instructions. The assistant then briefs the player(s) concerned and sends him to the table. This procedure has allowed the coach an almost unbroken span of attention on the game itself, and yet a very full preparation of substitutes, and analysis of player performance. It demands, obviously, an extremely good co-operation between coach and assistant, including efficient communication. For a player coach hoping to be successful at higher levels of play, having a good assistant coach on the bench is virtually imperative.

It is just as necessary that the assistant coach should have the same kind of trust, faith and respect as is the case between all other members of the team. My own experience with assistant coaches has been mixed. Outstanding personnel in sport tend to have strong personality traits. The chances of blending two strong men into a 'coach and assistant team' are pretty slim unless the assistant has the very necessary quality of humility, and the coach possesses great tact and sympathy. My first attempts to co-operate with assistants failed, certainly because I was tactless in my treatment of my colleagues, and perhaps because they could not tolerate the dominant nature of my own personality. More recently I have found immense benefits at both club level (where as a player coach it was imperative for me to have an assistant) and international, by choosing an assistant of undenied ability and strong personality but who was still prepared to accept the 'lesser' role in coaching a national team. My remarks on page 241 concerning the joint effort of a star and his substitute apply even more so in the case of a coach and his assistant. A good assistant can be the making of a coach.

Conclusion

The patient reader will now have followed me through a complex and yet rational process, from basic fundamentals to balanced team play. Some of it must have seemed very simple, and perhaps some a little strange or difficult. My attempt has been to present what *is*, rather than my own opinions. The reader will have realised that, inevitably, I must fail to become completely dissociated from my own opinions. I apologise for this, but perhaps it has made the text a little more human, and more bearable.

There has been very little that the reader can take away and immediately apply in his own situation. Basic principles are not like that, they have then to be applied in specific situations. This is perhaps where I might hope, humbly, to form a team with the reader. My part to describe the basics, yours to decide how they should be fitted to *your* needs. If only for this reason, though actually for others as well, I hope you achieve great successes from the game. After all—that's why we play.

Index